RHYTHM FACTORING

RHYTHM
NOTATION
AND
DEXTERITY

APRIL LYNN

RHYTHM FACTORING

To request permissions, contact the publisher at aprillynncoaching@gmail.com

Paperback: 9798985719208
Library of Congress Number: 9798985719208

First paperback edition May 2022
Editing and layout by April Lynn
Cover Art by April Lynn
Cover Design by Amanda Costello

Printed in the USA by Village Books.

Published by April Lynn
Website: APRILLYNNCOACHING.COM

For additional educational resources related to this material, contact the author or visit our website.

RHYTHM FACTORING

TABLE OF CONTENTS

INTRODUCTION

Rhythm Factoring is a notation method designed to increase hand-eye coordination and rhythm versatility and to expand abilities with hand percussion instruments. This method also develops pattern prediction while increasing confidence in improvisation and fusion styles. It can be played with any style of music or no music at all.

This course is based on basic concepts that can be learned by most anyone. It is a similar process to learning multiplication tables or pre-algebraic equations. The name Rhythm Factoring results from the development of the method as a parallel to teaching simple number factoring concepts to grade-school children.

In addition to musical applications, Rhythm Factoring increases mental skills associated with quick math, pattern recognition, and projection. The notation method cultivates a visual understanding of pattern possibilities. Rhythm tables focus mental attention through pattern arrangement of orderly numeric combinations, like scales or drill patterns.

Another benefit of Rhythm Factoring is the development of bimanual dexterity, training intended toward becoming more ambidextrous. Throughout the course, the ordering of factors switches from right-hand to left-hand dominance. Switching lead hands encourages balance in handedness, increasing competence for the non-dominant hand, and quickening hand-eye coordination for both dominant and non-dominant hands.

Rhythm Factoring is not based on traditional music theory, yet it offers a fresh look at simple pattern arrangement as the basis for complex and intricate musical possibilities. Rhythm Factoring can benefit beginners and progressing musicians, as well as non-musicians who wish to develop bi-manual functioning, hand-eye coordination, quick math skills, pattern projection, numeric reasoning and more.

BACKGROUND

RHYTHM INSPIRATION

Rhythm Factoring was inspired by musical patterns learned in community belly dance classes. Various teachers offered basic patterns to be played with finger cymbals or hand drums, while accompanying basic dance steps. These were simple, common rhythms, played by dancers in the community. Teachers often handed out sheets with basic names for the notes written in outline form, with no indication of the length or notes, the time signature of the song, or the rest spacing between notes.

When I began teaching my own dance classes, I found it helpful to put basic patterns in a table format, to make it easier for students to clearly understand and practice the patterns, and to practice at home. I then expanded the method to create original rhythm patterns-adding new number patterns, arranging notes in different order, and changing accents.

INNOVATION AND IMPROVISATION

There is no right or wrong rhythm. Sounds can carry emotion and cultural or personal associations. Stories can be encoded into music through instrument, voice, gesture, and movement to transmit deep layers of meaning. Music, as a part of culture, is an evolving form of human expression influenced by a multitude of factors.. Rhythm Factoring explores music as a mathematical innovation, allowing form to direct function. Once the eye is trained to read the tables, the hands can develop muscular response to follow along- faster and more complex rhythmic patterns can then be learned easily.

METRONOME

While it is easiest to learn these rhythms with the help of a teacher, it is not necessary to have first-hand instruction, but it is helpful to use a metronome to learn to count rhythm. These simple mechanical devices are widely available in music store or online. As the needle swings from side to side, the clicking sound creates a measure of timing to help set the pace for musical practices. The timing can be set to a slow pace in the beginning and gradually increased over time. This is particularly helpful with complicated patterns and syncopated rhythms, as the notes do not fall on the beat and the accents are often silent. Hearing a metronome allows for faster reading and can be set to the third note in each table cell corresponding to the counted beats of each measure.

HOW TO USE THIS BOOK

UNDERSTANDING RHYTHM FACTORING- This section introduces terms, tables, symbols, notation, and rules for counting rhythms- priming the mind to understand the rest of the book and serving as a reference throughout the course.

SECTION-BY-SECTION OVERVIEW- These pages cover core concepts of the nine sections of the book, showing how the method progresses through increasingly complicated concepts, each section building on the most basic section. It is not necessary to complete every section in order. All sections build off the basics, but they do not otherwise build off each other. The exception is the Rhythm library. This collection of simplistic rhythm songs contains songs corresponding to each section and can be practiced after all other sections are completed, or it can be used as a practice supplement throughout the course.

SECTION PROGRESSION

BEGINNER Introducing basic factors- foundation for other sections
BASIC FACTORS- All further sections build off the basic factors

INTERMEDIATE Adding complexity to basic rhythms
ACCENTS- Standard accent and two variations layered over top of Basic Rhythms
DRUM NOTATION-Hand-drum notation layered over Basic Rhythms DOOM TEK KA

ADVANCED Adding challenging new rhythms and practices
SYNCOPATION- New silent emphasis patterns with pause symbol introduced
TIMING VARIATION- Waltzish 6 BEAT rhythm patterns
BIMANUAL DEXTERITY- Practice tables for balanced handedness

INTEGRATION SECTION- Practice songs to supplement each section,
RHYTHM LIBRARY section by section songs- formatted collection of simple phrases

EMBODIMENT SECTION Group circle dance
FINGER CYMBAL DANCE- Introducing simple dance steps and corresponding rhythm patterns for an embodied Rhythm Factoring experience.

UNDERSTANDING RHYTHM FACTORING

BASIC RHYTHM PATTERNS
Basic 3's
3-5-5
7-7
3-3-7
3-1-3-1-3

SYMBOLS   R= RIGHT   L= LEFT   * = REST   ^ = PAUSE   __ = ACCENT

Rhythm notation relies on a few simple symbols.
Each symbol represents either a played note or an un-played note.
The symbols of played notes are R L.
Un-played notes may be either a rest or a pause.   * REST   ^ PAUSE
An accent is indicated by underlying a symbol.   __ ACCENT

SYMBOLS- NOTATION
R :RIGHT,
L: LEFT,
*   REST,
^   PAUSE,
__ ACCENT

FACTORS
A "factor" is a combination of two or more notes. Each factor contains one or more played notes and one rest. SYNCOPATED factors also contain a silent pause note which holds the accent. The factors in this book are not the only possibilities, but a foundation for further variations.

BASIC FACTORS
3's - RLR* or LRL*
1's- R* or L*
5's - RLRLR* or LRLRL*
7's - RLRLRLR* or LRLRLRL*

SYNCOPATED FACTORS
2's - RR^* - or LL^*
4's - RL^LR* - or LR^RL*

UNDERSTANDING RHYTHM FACTORING

PATTERNS

Factor Patterns are made by combining several factors. For most of this Teaching method, we are using the 4/4-time signature, and so the patterns must all add up to equal 16 notes. That is four quarter notes played in segments of 4 Sixteenth notes each. There are many pattern possibilities beyond those included in this book.

BASIC PATTERNS

      3-5-5- RLR * RLRLR * RLRLR * or LRL * LRLRL * LRLRL *
      3-3-7- RLR * RLR * RLRLRLR * or LRL * LRL * LRLRLRL *
      3-1-3-1-3- RLR * R * RLR * R * RLR .....

SYNCOPATED PATTERNS

      3-4-4- RLR * RL^LR * RL^LR * or LRL * LR^RL * LR^RL *
      2-4-4- RR^* RL^LR * RL^LR * or LL^ * LR^RL * LR^RL *
      2-3-4-1- RR^ * RLR * RL^LR * R * or LL^ * LRL * LR^RL * L *

PHRASING

In addition to factors and patterns, rhythms are arranged into phrases, patterns strung together to create a longer musical structure.

SONG BUILDING

The rhythm songs in this course are constructed using a simple song-building method. This is not just an ordering of numbers, but a system of pattern arrangement that can communicate mood, story, and emotion; music is built on numbers. These simple songs contain two verses, with three pattern combinations each, and two choruses, with two pattern combinations each, plus a finishing phrase. Choruses are more repetitive; verses are more lyrical.

UNDERSTANDING RHYTHM FACTORING

COUNTING FACTORS

Rhythm patterns are combinations of numbers totaling sixteen beats, consisting of played or un-played notes. In 4x4 time signature, there is one whole note per measure, four quarter notes per measure, 16 sixteenth notes per measure. We do not play all the notes, but the silent spaces are counted as a beat. The REST symbol * is assigned for standard silent beats.

TABLE FORMAT

Tables consist of one column naming the pattern- (3-3-7, etc.) followed by four columns of factors, with four symbols per column representing a quarter of a measure each.

TIMING VARIATION

The section on timing variation is the exception to this 16 beat rule. All patterns in that section are combination of number totaling 24 beats, based on the possibilities of 6x8 time signature.

STANDARD PATTERNS TOTAL 16

How many times can each factor fit into a measure of 16 notes?

Some factors cannot fit evenly and must be combined with other factors to equal sixteen.

Singles into 16 = 16 (no rests or pauses in singles)

1 factor into 16 = 8 (one rest, two notes total per 1 factor)

2 factor into 16 =4 (one rest and one pause, four notes total per 2 factor)

3 factor into 16 = 4 (one rest each, four notes per 3 factor)

4 factor into 16 = 2.5 (one rest and one pause, six notes per 4 factor)

5 factor into 16 = 2.5 (one rest, six notes per 5 factor)

7 factor into 16 = 2 (one rest, eight notes per 7 factor)

UNDERSTANDING RHYTHM FACTORING

READING 16TH NOTES

Learn to translate the notation with the following phrase
"AND A-ONE-E, AND A-TWO-E, AND A-THREE-E, AND A-FOUR-E"

PHRASE READING

    N = "AND"
    A = "A"
    1 = "ONE"
    Y = "E"

Examples

```
3 - 3 - 3 - 3     R L R *        R L R *      R L R *      R L R *
                  N A 1 Y        N A 2 Y      N A 3 Y      N A 4 Y


3 - 3 - 7         R L R *        R L R *      R L R L R L R *
                  N A 1 Y        N A 2 Y      N A 3 Y N A 4 Y


3 - 5 - 5         R L R *      R L R L R *      R L R L R *
                  N A 1 Y      N A 2 Y N A      3 Y N A 4 Y


3 - 1 - 3 - 1 - 3  R L R *     R *     R L     R *    R *     R L R *
                  N A 1 Y      N A    2 Y      N A    3 Y     N A 4 Y


5 - 1 - 5 - 1     R L R L R *     R *      R L R L R *     R *
                  N A 1 Y N A     2 Y      N A 3 Y N A     4 Y


3 - 4 - 4         R L R *      R L ^ L R *    R L      ^ L R *
                  N A 1 Y      N A 2 Y N A    3 Y      N A 4 Y
```

UNDERSTANDING RHYTHM FACTORING

RULE OF ODDS AND EVENS

Odd factors = sum of numbers + 1 for the REST *
Even factors = sum of numbers + 1 for each PAUSE ^ + 1 for each REST *
    Add one silent pause note to the even-numbered pattern plus the regular rest
    Turn all evens into odds by including a silent pause accent note

In 4/4 Time Signature when each played note is a sixteenth note
    A measure has four quarter notes represented by individual cells in the tables
    That makes 16 sixteenth notes per measure, four notes per cell, four cells per line
    Count sixteenth notes using the following phrase

"AND A ONE Y" "AND A TWO Y" "AND A THREE Y" "AND A FOUR Y"
  1   2   3   4   5   6   7   8   9   10   11   12   13 14 15 16

COUNTING FACTORS WITH RULE OF ODDS AND EVENS

Factor 1 = 2 Notes – played- R *
Factor 3 = 4 Notes – played- R L R *
Factor 5 = 6 Notes – played- R L R L R *
Factor 7 = 8 Notes – played- R L R L R L R
Factor 4 = 6 Notes – played- R L ^ L R *
Factor 2 = 4 Notes – played- R R ^ *
All factor patterns must then add to sixteen

SYNCOPATED FACTORS COMBINE WITH BASIC FACTORS TO TOTAL 16

3*4*4*	4*1*7*
3 = 4 Notes	4 = 6 Notes
4 = 6 Notes	1 = 2 Notes
4 = 6 Notes_	7 = 8 Notes
Total 16	**Total 16**

UNDERSTANDING RHYTHM FACTORING

FACTORS AND PLACES

A simple formula for seeing the potential in pattern expansion
Pattern variations can be made by changing the order of factors.

All patterns with two or more factors can be combined in new order to make variations

The number of variations depends on two things:

1. How many factors are used?

2. How many places are occupied?

All combinations total sixteen including rests and syncopation pauses

EXAMPLES

5-1-5-1 has four places and two factors (5 and 1) making 6 possible rows

3-5-1-3 has four places but three factors (5,3, and 1) making 12 possible rows

3-5-5	2 factors, 3 places = 3 rows
3-3-7	2 factors, 3 places = 3 rows
3-1-3-1-3	2 factors, 5 places = 9 rows
5-1-5-1	2 factors, 4 places = 6 rows
3-5-1-3	3 factors, 4 places = 12 rows
3-1-3-1-1-1	2 factors, 6 places = 15 rows
3-4-4	2 factors, 3 places = 3 rows
3-1-2-4	4 factors, 4 places= ?

SECTION-BY-SECTION OVERVIEW

SECTION 1
BASIC FACTORS

Introducing **RHYTHM FACTORING**. Begin with a basic understanding of formatted symbols. The tables present each factor phrase in a way that is readable and predictable. This is a path to learning many complicated rhythm patterns from this method. This first section is a primer section- beginning with simple **BASIC FACTORS**, then combining these factors into variations.

BASIC PATTERNS- made by combining several basic factors into a sequence. Each combination of factors can be further varied be simply reordering the factors within the patterns. In this way, each simple pattern blossoms into a table, or family of related patterns, each with unique sound.

First, simple combinations are introduced- 3's are the most basic factors. By combining 3's with the other basic factors (5,1,7) the basic patterns are introduced one at a time. Throughout this section, each new combination of factors is followed by a new table showing many ordering possibilities within the **PATTERN FAMILY**.

Based on standard 4/4 timing, the basic patterns are all **16 BEAT TABLES**- the must all add up to equal 16 sixteenth notes. Each line of the tables contains one title column, followed by four columns each representing one quarter note in the measure. The quarter note cells are divided into four symbols. Learning to read and play these basic factors and patterns becomes the foundation for learning all other material in this course.

SECTION CONTENTS

INTRODUCTION TO BASIC FACTORING
SYMBOLS/ NOTATION
BASIC FACTORS
BASIC PATTERNS

SECTION-BY-SECTION OVERVIEW

SECTION 2
ACCENT VARIATIONS

An **ACCENT** can be added to a note to give it more emphasis by underlining the symbol of that note. Accent placement determines which notes are played slightly louder than others. In most cases, the accent falls on the last fragment of the factor unless otherwise indicated. This is what we call a **STANDARD ACCENT**. Accenting offers a way of punctuating a rhythmic phrase.

When the accent falls on any other factor than the standard accents, this is an **ACCENT VARIATION**. An accent falling on the first note of the factor is called a **REVERSE ACCENT**. When the accent lands in the middle note of a factor it is called a **CENTER ACCENT**. Accent variations can happen at any time, adding character and uniqueness to the interpretation of rhythmic patterns.

Varying the placement of accent within factors creates a different rhythm feeling. Accents hold the emotional emphasis of a song. Creating meaning through storytelling and expression, turning sounds into music. There is no right or wrong way to emphasize sound, but it is significant to note the encoding of cultural and emotional content that is possible. Accent changes music as much as it changes speech-variation on the English language based on regional dialect, individual speech habits, context, and other influences.

SECTION CONTENTS

INTRODUCTION TO ACCENTS
STANDARD ACCENT
ACCENT VARIATIONS

SECTION-BY-SECTION OVERVIEW

SECTION 3
HAND DRUM NOTATION

The rhythm notes **DOOM TEK** and **KA** are common in various parts the world. **DOOM TEK** and **KA** are basic three notes of hand drumming. The first note- **DOOM**- is played with the right hand in the center of the drum and represents the accented note of a rhythm pattern. The second note **TEK** is also played by the right hand, but on the rim of the drum. The third note **KA** is played by the left hand, also on the rim of the drum.

Rhythm Factoring works very well with drum notation. Simply replace all DOOM and TEK notes with right hand notation, underlining all the DOOM notes because a DOOM corresponds to an accented right-hand note in a right-hand dominant phrasing. Then replace all KA notes with left-hand notation. This process instantly converts drum songs into rhythm table format. Any pattern from the Rhythm Factoring method can be played according to this simple three-note approach by reversing the notation process.

TYPES OF HAND DRUMS
There are many types of hand drums from all over the world. Any surface can be used for hand-drumming, though some surfaces make little sound. Hand drumming can be practiced on the legs, or a table surface, any time the two hands are the main tools of percussion.
Having a round flexible surface allows for the three distinct notes to be played clearly, as an edge creates a different sound than the center, but if you are practicing on a surface with no give, the Doom notes can be created by cupping the palm and smacking the surface with the whole surface of the cupped hand, while the Tek and Ka notes are played with the base of the fingers slapping the surface edge.

SECTION CONTENTS
INTRODUCTION TO DRUM NOTATION
COMMON DRUM NOTES
DOOM AND ACCENT VARIATIONS
FACTORING DRUM NOTES

SECTION-BY-SECTION OVERVIEW

SECTION 4
SYNCOPATION

SYNCOPATED RHYTHMS are created by accenting a silent note. This pause note carrying the accent is assigned the symbol (^). Hold the pause like an elevated suspense. Syncopated rhythms have a feeling of anticipation, full of energy and mystery.

The **SYNCOPATED 4** accent is on the un-played note between four played notes in the sequence **RL^LR***. This factor holds six sixteenth notes, or six places in a sixteen-beat table. The first two notes are played RL. The middle note carrying the accent is assigned the symbol ^, then the final notes are played LR and SYNCOPATED 4 is always followed by a silent note marked * .

Speak the phrase- "**right, left ^ left right** * starting with a low pitch "right" and lift your pitch "left." Hold the center pause like an elevated suspense, then start high again "left and drop pitch down again "right."

SYNCOPATED 2 accent also lands on an un-played note just after the two played notes in the sequence **RR^***. This rhythm occupies four sixteenth notes and may be played on its own as straight two's or paired with other factors to form patterns equaling 16 sixteenth notes. The two played notes are played one after the other. The pause note is still part of the numeric piece and SYNCOPATED 2 is always followed by a silent note marked *

Speak the phrase- "**right, right ^** * "**right, right ^** *. Starting with a swift abrupt double sound with a stomping feeling. Hold the pause note in elevated suspense, then hold the rest note resolving the suspense.

SECTION CONTENTS
INTRODUCTION TO SYNCOPATION
SYNCOPATED 4 AND SYNCOPATED 3
COUNTING SYNCOPATED RHYTHMS
SPEAKING SYNCOPATED RHYTHMS

SECTION-BY-SECTION OVERVIEW

SECTION 6
TIMING VARIATION

TIME SIGNATURE

Time Signature is an aspect of rhythm measuring of beats per measure throughout a song. Musical complexity is enhanced through timing variations. Subtle changes in timing create wonderful variations to the feeling, mood, and character of the music.

Popular music is often written in **4/4-TIME SIGNATURE**- 4 quarter notes per measure, a whole note is one measure. Most of this course deals with this common time signature.

Variations in Time Signature are common in some musical genres. A familiar variation example is a **6/8 VARIATION** which has a floating waltzy feeling. This collection of rhythms is arranged in **24 BEAT TABLES**.

The feeling of six beat timing is delightful, just a simple change in numeric patterning creates a completely new music using the same simple patterns. There is a significant difference to the feeling created by this music, the vast potential for expression through music.

Rhythm Factoring can be applied to other time signatures as well. A few interesting time signatures to consider include 9/8 or 10/8.

SECTION CONTENTS
INTRODUCTION TO TIME SIGNATURES
TIME SIGNATURE VARIATIONS
STANDARD AND VARIATION 6/8

SECTION-BY-SECTION OVERVIEW

SECTION 7
BIMANUAL DEXTERITY

HANDEDNESS, also known as **HAND DOMINANCE,** has an impact on how we learn to use our hands throughout life. While many people experience a dominant hand from childhood, it is possible to develop the non-dominant hand, and even to become **AMBIDEXTROUS**- equal in both hands. **BI-MANUAL COMPETENCE** can be nurtured so that simple tasks like eating can be done with either hand. Developing muscular control in the non-dominant hand can increase productivity. Many activities in life would be much easier if we were able to rely equally on both hands.

Rhythm is a concept of the mind. Pattern interpretation happens in our mental arrangement of numbers. This process does not happen in the hands, but when learning to play percussion instruments, hand dominance becomes relevant and amplified. Bi-Manual Dexterity practice can develop symmetrical competence with both hands. By learning to play the instrument equally with both hands, more possibilities can be generated.

Though most people seem to be born with a naturally dominant side, this dominance is reinforced throughout life. Each time we choose to use our dominant hand because it is more convenient, rather than training the non-dominant hand to do the same task, we deepen the mental connections with the dominant side. All the while, we neglect the development that is possible for the non-dominant side. Bi-manual dexterity helps to balance handedness, developing symmetry in the muscle memory of both hands, cultivating brain-to-hand messaging system and hand-eye coordination for both dominant and non-dominant hands.

SECTION CONTENTS
INTRODUCTION TO BI-MANUAL DEXTERITY
LINE BY LINE TABLES
FACTOR BY FACTOR TABLES

SECTION-BY-SECTION OVERVIEW

SECTION 8
RHYTHM SONG LIBRARY

The **RHYTHM SONG LIBRARY** offers a complete collection of Teaching songs corresponding to the **LEVEL-BY-LEVEL** learning approach followed in this book. The songs in this library are simple constructions, offered to reiterate the concepts of factoring for deeper understanding and retention. By playing rhythm factors in a simple song format, comprehension is improved. Meanwhile, hand-eye coordination improves through the introduction of arrangement complexity as well as repetition.

The Song Library can either be played song by song after completing the entire course, as an **OVERALL REVIEW** or the songs can be learned and played along with the related lessons as an **INTEGRATION EXERCISE** along the way. Each song in the library is labeled according to the Section in which the relevant factors were introduced.

For best results, use the song library as an integration exercise after completing the corresponding section. Play through the songs associated with the completed section and review the songs from previously completed sections. When all sections are complete, most of the song library will be familiar. Play through the full library again from start to finish, as a final exercise to cement the learning of the entire course.

The song library also contains the rhythm accompaniment to the Finger Cymbal Dance. Though the Finger Cymbal Dance is not introduced until the following section, it is advisable to play though the Finger Cymbal Dance music separately before learning the dance and playing along.

SECTION CONTENTS
INTRODUCTION TO THE RHYTHM SONG LIBRARY
SONG BUILDING METHOD
PHRASING
SONG SHAPING
SONG LIBRARY

SECTION-BY-SECTION OVERVIEW

SECTION 9
FINGER CYMBAL DANCE

The **FINGER CYMBAL DANCE** is a traveling circle group dance performed with three or more dancers. **FINGER CYMBAL PATTERNS** are paired with basic group dance forms. Some figures require simple **FRAMING** of the arms around the face according to the shape created by the steps. Additional complexity result from **TAPPING** one hand into the other, or by tapping another dancer's finger cymbals, or **MUFFLING** the finger cymbal with the hand.

These patterns require coordination and are best learned after carefully practicing both the steps and the finger symbol patterns independently. It is also worthwhile for each dancer to learn the **COORDINATED FIGURES** individually before attempting to move together with the group circle. It is helpful to have a **CALLER-** someone who is not participating in the dance to watch the positioning of the circle and "call" **TRANSITIONS** from one figure to the next.

The dance is a fun and satisfying way to embody these rhythms and enjoy this creative sound project. The group rapport will grow as coupling patterns and movement transitions create a flow of energy among the members of the circle. This is a great completion to any finger cymbal practice session as well as a satisfying final project at the end of rhythm training.

SECTION CONTENTS
INTRODUCTION TO FINGER CYMBAL DANCE
GROUP CIRCLE FORMS
DANCE CALLER
DANCE FORMATIONS
FRAMING ARM POSTURES
SPECIAL FINGER CYMBAL TONES

SECTION 1

BASIC FACTORS

BASIC FACTORS

INTRODUCTION TO BASIC FACTORING
Basic factors are introduced in simple groups, one level at a time.

BASIC SYMBOLS/ NOTATION
Basic patterns are made of three primary symbols, each symbol represents either a played note, or an un-played rest.

BASIC SYMBOLS **R = RIGHT** **L = LEFT** *** = REST**

BASIC FACTORS
Basic factors contain several notes and one rest
- 3's   RLR* or LRL*
- 1's   R* or L*
- 5's   RLRLR* or LRLRL*
- 7's   RLRLRLR* or LRLRLRL*

BASIC PATTERNS
Basic Patterns are made by combining several basic factors. First, we learn simple combinations- 3's are the most basic factors. By combining 3's with the other basic factors (5,1,7) the basic patterns are introduced one at a time. Patterns all add up to equal 16 Sixteenth notes= 4 quarter notes= 1 whole note.

3-5-5	RLR*RLRLR*RLRLR*	or	LRL*LRLRL*LRLRL*
3-3-7	RLR*RLR*RLRLRLR*	or	LRL*LRL*LRLRLRL*
3-1-3-1-3	RLR*R*RLR*R*RLR*	or	LRL*L*LRL*L*LRL*

BASIC FACTORS LESSON BY LESSON
LESSON ONE- Introducing Basic Factors
LESSON TWO- Factor by Factor- Right
LESSON THREE- Factor by Factor- Left
LESSON FOUR- Factor Combinations- Right
LESSON FIVE- Factor Combinations- Left

BASIC FACTORS

LESSON ONE
INTRODUCING BASIC PATTERNS

RIGHT HAND

3*3*3*3*	R L R *	R L R *	R L R *	R L R *

7*7*	R L R L	R L R *	R L R L	R L R *

3*3*7*	R L R *	R L R *	R L R L	R L R *

3*1*3*1*3*	R L R *	R * R L	R * R *	R L R *

3*5*5*	R L R *	R L R L	R * R L	R L R *

1*3*1*1*1*3	R * R L	R * R *	R * R *	R L R *

5*1*5*1*	R L R L	R * R *	R L R L	R * R *

7*1*5*	R L R L	R L R *	R * R L	R L R *

3*5*1*3*	R L R *	R L R L	R * R *	R L R *

3*1*7*1*	R L R *	R * R L	R L R L	R * R *

3*1*1*5*1*	R L R *	R * R *	R L R L	R * R *

BASIC FACTORS

LESSON ONE
INTRODUCING BASIC PATTERNS

LEFT HAND

3*3*3*3*	L R L *	L R L *	L R L *	L R L *

7*7*	L R L R	L R L *	L R L R	L R L *

3*3*7*	L R L *	L R L *	L R L R	L R L *

3*1*3*1*3*	L R L *	L * L R	L * L *	L R L *

3*5*5*	L R L *	L R L R	L * L R	L R L *

1*3*1*1*1*3	L * L R	L * L *	L * L *	L R L *

5*1*5*1*	L R L R	L * L *	L R L R	L * L *

7*1*5*	L R L R	L R L *	L * L R	L R L *

3*5*1*3*	L R L *	L R L R	L * L *	L R L *

3*1*7*1*	L R L *	L * L R	L R L R	L * L *

3*1*1*5*1*	L R L *	L * L *	L R L R	L * L *

BASIC FACTORS

LESSON TWO
FACTOR BY FACTOR RIGHT HAND

BASIC 3'S RIGHT HAND

3*3*3*3*	R L R *	R L R *	R L R *	R L R *
3*3*3*3*	R L R *	R L R *	R L R *	R L R *

DOUBLE 7'S RIGHT HAND

7*7*	R L R L	R L R *	R L R L	R L R *
7*7*	R L R L	R L R *	R L R L	R L R *

3-3-7 RIGHT HAND

3*3*7*	R L R *	R L R *	R L R L	R L R *
3*7*3*	R L R *	R L R L	R L R *	R L R *
7*3*3*	R L R L	R L R *	R L R *	R L R *

3-1-3-1-3 RIGHT HAND

3*1*3*1*3*	R L R *	R * R L	R * R *	R L R *
1*3*3*1*3*	R * R L	R * R L	R * R *	R L R *
1*3*1*3*3*	R * R L	R * R *	R L R *	R L R *
3*3*1*3*1*	R L R *	R L R *	R * R L	R * R *
3*1*3*3*1*	R L R *	R * R L	R * R L	R * R *
1*1*3*3*3*	R * R *	R L R *	R L R *	R L R *
3*1*1*3*3*	R L R *	R * R *	R L R *	R L R *
3*3*1*1*3*	R L R *	R L R *	R * R *	R L R *

BASIC FACTORS

LESSON TWO
FACTOR BY FACTOR RIGHT HAND

3-5-5 RIGHT HAND

3*5*5*	R L R *	R L R L	R * R L	R L R *
5*3*5*	R L R L	R * R L	R * R L	R L R *
5*5*3*	R L R L	R * R L	R L R *	R L R *

1-3-1-1-1-3 RIGHT HAND

1*3*1*1*1*3	R * R L	R * R *	R * R *	R L R *
1*1*1*3*1*3	R * R *	R * R L	R * R *	R L R *
1*1*1*3*3*1	R * R *	R * R L	R * R L	R * R *
1*1*1*1*3*3	R * R *	R * R *	R L R *	R L R *
1*1*3*3*1*1	R * R *	R L R *	R L R *	R * R *
1*1*3*1*3*1	R * R *	R L R *	R * R L	R * R *
1*1*3*1*1*3	R * R *	R L R *	R * R *	R L R *
1*3*1*1*1*3	R * R L	R * R *	R * R *	R L R *
1*3*1*1*3*1	R * R L	R * R *	R * R L	R * R *
1*3*3*1*1*1	R * R L	R * R L	R * R *	R * R *
3*1*1*1*1*3	R L R *	R * R *	R * R *	R L R *
3*1*1*1*3*1	R L R*	R * R *	R * R L	R * R *
3*1*1*3*1*1	R L R *	R * R *	R L R *	R * R *
3*1*3*1*1*1	R L R *	R * R L	R * R *	R * R *

BASIC FACTORS

LESSON THREE
FACTOR BY FACTOR LEFT HAND

BASIC 3'S LEFT HAND

3*3*3*3*	L R L *	L R L *	L R L *	L R L *
3*3*3*3*	L R L *	L R L *	L R L *	L R L *

DOUBLE 7'S LEFT HAND

7*7*	L R L R	L R L *	L R L R	L R L *
7*7*	L R L R	L R L *	L R L R	L R L *

3-3-7 LEFT HAND

3*3*7*	L R L *	L R L *	L R L R	L R L *
3*7*3*	L R L *	L R L R	L R L *	L R L *
7*3*3*	L R L R	L R L *	L R L *	L R L *

3-1-3-1-3 LEFT HAND

3*1*3*1*3*	L R L *	L * L R	L * L *	L R L *
1*3*3*1*3*	L * L R	L * L R	L * L *	L R L *
1*3*1*3*3*	L * L R	L * L *	L R L *	L R L *
3*3*1*3*1*	L R L *	L R L *	L * L R	L * L *
3*1*3*3*1*	L R L *	L * L R	L * L R	L * L *
1*1*3*3*3*	L * L *	L R L *	L R L *	L R L *
3*1*1*3*3*	L R L *	L * L *	L R L *	L R L *
3*3*1*1*3*	L R L *	L R L *	L * L *	L R L *

BASIC FACTORS

LESSON THREE
FACTOR BY FACTOR LEFT HAND

3-5-5 LEFT HAND

3*5*5*	L R L *	L R L R	L * L R	L R L *
5*3*5*	L R L R	L * L R	L * L R	L R L *
5*5*3*	L R L R	L * L R	L R L *	L R L *

1-3-1-1-1-3 LEFT HAND

1*3*1*1*1*3	L * L R	L * L *	L * L *	L R L *
1*1*1*3*1*3	L * L *	L * L R	L * L *	L R L *
1*1*1*3*3*1	L * L *	L * L R	L * L R	L * L *
1*1*1*1*3*3	L * L *	L * L *	L R L *	L R L *
1*1*3*3*1*1	L * L *	L R L *	L R L *	L * L *
1*1*3*1*3*1	L * L *	L R L *	L * L R	L * L *
1*1*3*1*1*3	L * L *	L R L *	L * L *	L R L *
1*3*1*1*1*3	L * L R	L * L *	L * L *	L R L *
1*3*1*1*3*1	L * L R	L * L *	L * L R	L * L *
1*3*3*1*1*1	L * L R	L * L R	L * L *	L * L *
3*1*1*1*1*3	L R L *	L * L *	L * L *	L R L *
3*1*1*1*3*1	L R L *	L * L *	L * L R	L * L *
3*1*1*3*1*1	L R L *	L * L *	L R L *	L * L *
3*1*3*1*1*1	L R L *	L * L R	L * L *	L * L *

BASIC FACTORS

LESSON FOUR
COMBINED FACTORS RIGHT HAND

5-1-5-1 RIGHT HAND

5*1*5*1*	R L R L	R * R *	R L R L	R * R *
5*1*1*5*	R L R L	R * R *	R * R L	R L R *
5*5*1*1*	R L R L	R * R L	R L R *	R * R *
1*1*5*5*	R * R *	R L R L	R * R L	R L R *
1*5*1*5*	R * R L	R L R *	R * R L	R L R *
1*5*5*1*	R * R L	R L R *	R L R L	R * R *

7-1-5 RIGHT HAND

7*1*5*	R L R L	R L R *	R * R L	R L R *
7*5*1*	R L R L	R L R *	R L R L	R * R *
5*7*1*	R L R L	R * R L	R L R L	R * R *
5*1*7*	R L R L	R * R *	R L R L	R L R *
1*7*5*	R * R L	R L R L	R * R L	R L R *
1*5*7*	R * R L	R L R *	R L R L	R L R *

BASIC FACTORS

LESSON FOUR
COMBINED FACTORS RIGHT HAND

3-5-1-3 RIGHT HAND

3*5*1*3*	R L R *	R L R L	R * R *	R L R *
5*1*3*3*	R L R L	R * R *	R L R *	R L R *
1*3*3*5*	R * R L	R * R L	R * R L	R L R *
1*3*5*3*	R * R L	R * R L	R L R *	R L R *
1*5*3*3*	R * R L	R L R *	R L R *	R L R *
5*3*3*1*	R L R L	R * R L	R * R L	R * R *
5*3*1*3*	R L R L	R * R L	R * R *	R L R *
3*1*5*3*	R L R *	R * R L	R L R *	R L R *
3*3*1*5*	R L R *	R L R *	R * R L	R L R *
3*5*3*1*	R L R *	R L R L	R * R L	R * R *

3-1-7-1 RIGHT HAND

3*1*7*1*	R L R *	R * R L	R L R L	R * R *
3*1*1*7*	R L R *	R * R *	R L R L	R L R *
3*7*1*1*	R L R *	R L R L	R L R *	R * R *
7*1*1*3*	R L R L	R L R *	R * R *	R L R *
7*1*3*1*	R L R L	R L R *	R * R L	R * R *
7*3*1*1*	R L R L	R L R *	R L R *	R * R *
1*3*7*1*	R * R L	R * R L	R L R L	R * R *
1*3*1*7*	R * R L	R * R *	R L R L	R L R *
1*7*1*3*	R * R L	R L R L	R * R *	R L R *

BASIC FACTORS

LESSON FOUR
COMBINED FACTORS RIGHT HAND

3-1-1-5-1 RIGHT HAND

3*1*1*5*1*	R L R *	R * R *	R L R L	R * R *
3*1*1*1*5*	R L R *	R * R *	R * R L	R L R *
3*1*5*1*1*	R L R *	R * R L	R L R *	R * R *
3*5*1*1*1*	R L R *	R L R L	R * R *	R * R *
5*3*1*1*1*	R L R L	R * R L	R * R *	R * R *
5*1*1*1*3*	R L R L	R * R *	R * R *	R L R *
5*1*1*3*1*	R L R L	R * R *	R * R L	R * R *
5*1*3*1*1*	R L R L	R * R *	R L R *	R * R *
1*5*1*1*3*	R * R L	R L R *	R * R *	R L R *
1*5*1*3*1*	R * R L	R L R *	R * R L	R * R *
1*5*3*1*1*	R * R L	R L R *	R L R *	R * R *
1*3*5*1*1*	R * R L	R * R L	R L R *	R * R *
1*3*1*1*5*	R * R L	R * R *	R * R L	R L R *
1*3*1*5*1*	R * R L	R * R *	R L R L	R * R *
1*1*5*3*1*	R * R *	R L R L	R * R L	R * R *
1*1*5*1*3*	R * R *	R L R L	R * R *	R L R *
1*1*3*5*1*	R * R *	R L R *	R L R L	R * R *
1*1*3*1*5*	R * R *	R L R *	R * R L	R L R *
1*1*1*3*5*	R * R *	R * R L	R * R L	R L R *

BASIC FACTORS

LESSON FIVE
COMBINED FACTORS LEFT HAND

5-1-5-1 LEFT HAND

5*1*5*1*	L R L R	L * L *	L R L R	L * L *
5*1*1*5*	L R L R	L * L *	L * L R	L R L *
5*5*1*1*	L R L R	L * L R	L R L *	L * L *
1*1*5*5*	L * L *	L R L R	L * L R	L R L *
1*5*1*5*	L * L R	L R L *	L * L R	L R L *
1*5*5*1*	L * L R	L R L *	L R L R	L * L *

7-1-5 LEFT HAND

7*1*5*	L R L R	L R L *	L * L R	L R L *
7*5*1*	L R L R	L R L *	L R L R	L * L *
5*7*1*	L R L R	L * L R	L R L R	L * L *
5*1*7*	L R L R	L * L *	L R L R	L R L *
1*7*5*	L * L R	L R L R	L * L R	L R L *
1*5*7*	L * L R	L R L *	L R L R	L R L *

BASIC FACTORS

LESSON FIVE
COMBINED FACTORS LEFT HAND

3-5-1-3 LEFT HAND

3*5*1*3*	L R L *	L R L R	L * L *	L R L *
5*1*3*3*	L R L R	L * L *	L R L *	L R L *
1*3*3*5*	L * L R	L * L R	L * L R	L R L *
1*3*5*3*	L * L R	L * L R	L R L *	L R L *
1*5*3*3*	L * L R	L R L *	L R L *	L R L *
5*3*3*1*	L R L R	L * L R	L * L R	L * L *
5*3*1*3*	L R L R	L * L R	L * L *	L R L *
3*1*5*3*	L R L *	L * L R	L R L *	L R L *
3*3*1*5*	L R L *	L R L *	L * L R	L R L *
3*5*3*1*	L R L *	L R L R	L * L R	L * L *

3-1-7-1- LEFT HAND

3*1*7*1*	L R L *	L * L R	L R L R	L * L *
3*1*1*7*	L R L *	L * L *	L R L R	L R L *
3*7*1*1*	L R L *	L R L R	L R L *	L * L *
7*1*1*3*	L R L R	L R L *	L * L *	L R L *
7*1*3*1*	L R L R	L R L *	L * L R	L * L *
7*3*1*1*	L R L R	L R L *	L R L *	L * L *
1*3*7*1*	L * L R	L * L R	L R L R	L * L *
1*3*1*7*	L * L R	L * L *	L R L R	L R L *
1*7*1*3*	L * L R	L R L R	L * L *	L R L *

BASIC FACTORS

LESSON FIVE
COMBINED FACTORS LEFT HAND

3-1-1-5-1 LEFT HAND

3*1*1*5*1*	L R L *	L * L *	L R L R	L * L *
3*1*1*1*5*	L R L *	L * L *	L * L R	L R L *
3*1*5*1*1*	L R L *	L * L R	L R L *	L * L *
3*5*1*1*1*	L R L *	L R L R	L * L *	L * L *
5*3*1*1*1*	L R L R	L * L R	L * L *	L * L *
5*1*1*1*3*	L R L R	L * L *	L * L *	L R L *
5*1*1*3*1*	L R L R	L * L *	L * L R	L * L *
5*1*3*1*1*	L R L R	L * L *	L R L *	L * L *
1*5*1*1*3*	L * L R	L R L *	L * L *	L R L *
1*5*1*3*1*	L * L R	L R L *	L * L R	L * L *
1*5*3*1*1*	L * L R	L R L *	L R L *	L * L *
1*3*5*1*1*	L * L R	L * L R	L R L *	L * L *
1*3*1*1*5*	L * L R	L * L *	L * L R	L R L *
1*3*1*5*1*	L * L R	L * L *	L R L R	L * L *
1*1*5*3*1*	L * L *	L R L R	L * L R	L * L *
1*1*5*1*3*	L * L *	L R L R	L * L *	L R L *
1*1*3*5*1*	L * L *	L R L *	L R L R	L * L *
1*1*3*1*5*	L * L *	L R L *	L * L R	L R L *
1*1*1*3*5*	L * L *	L * L R	L * L R	L R L *

SECTION 2

ACCENT VARIATIONS

ACCENT VARIATIONS

INTRODUCTION TO ACCENTS
An accented note is a note in a factor which holds an extra emphasis, indicated by simple underlining. The note that is underlined is played slightly louder than others. Varying the placement of accents within factors creates different rhythmic feeling.

STANDARD ACCENT
In most cases, the accent falls on the last fragment of the factor, unless otherwise indicated. This is called a standard accent.

ACCENT VARIATIONS
When the accent falls on any other factor than the standard accents, this is an accent variation. An accent falling on the first note of the factor is called a reverse accent. When the accent lands in the middle note of a factor it is called a center accent.

Standard Accent- Accent falls on the last fragment of the factor.

RLR*   RLRLR*   RLRLRLR*

Variants- Accent falls on any other factor than the standard accents.
Reverse Accent- Accent falls on the first note of the factor
Center Accent- Accent falls on the middle not of the factor

Standard Accent	RL<u>R</u>*	RLRL<u>R</u>*	RLRLRL<u>R</u>*
Reverse Accent	<u>R</u>LR*	<u>R</u>LRLR*	<u>R</u>LRLRLR*
Center Accent	R<u>L</u>R	RL<u>R</u>LR*	RLRL<u>R</u>LR*

ACCENT VARIATIONS LESSON BY LESSON
LESSON ONE- Basic Pattern Accents Right and Left
LESSON TWO- Standard Accent Tables Right and Left
LESSON THREE- Reverse Accent Tables Right and Left
LESSON FOUR- Middle Accent Tables Right and Left

ACCENT VARIATIONS

LESSON ONE
BASIC PATTERN ACCENTS

BASIC PATTERNS
RIGHT HAND
STANDARD ACCENT- END NOTE

3*3*3*3*	R L <u>R</u> *	R L <u>R</u> *	R L <u>R</u> *	R L <u>R</u> *
3*3*7*	R L <u>R</u> *	R L <u>R</u> *	R L R L	R L <u>R</u> *
3*5*5*	R L <u>R</u> *	R L R L	<u>R</u> * R L	R L <u>R</u> *
7*7*	R L R L	R L <u>R</u> *	R L R L	R L <u>R</u> *
3*1*3*1*3*	R L <u>R</u> *	<u>R</u> * R L	<u>R</u> * <u>R</u> *	R L <u>R</u> *
5*1*5*1*	R L R L	<u>R</u> * <u>R</u> *	R L R L	<u>R</u> * <u>R</u> *
3*5*1*3*	R L <u>R</u> *	R L R L	<u>R</u> * <u>R</u> *	R L <u>R</u> *
3*1*7*1*	R L <u>R</u> *	<u>R</u> * R L	R L R L	<u>R</u> * <u>R</u> *
3*1*1*5*1*	R L <u>R</u> *	<u>R</u> * <u>R</u> *	R L R L	<u>R</u> * <u>R</u> *
7*1*5*	R L R L	R L <u>R</u> *	<u>R</u> * R L	R L <u>R</u> *

ACCENT VARIATIONS

LESSON ONE
BASIC PATTERN ACCENTS

BASIC PATTERNS
LEFT HAND
STANDARD ACCENTS- END NOTE

3*3*3*3*	L R L *	L R L *	L R L *	L R L *
3*3*7*	L R L *	L R L *	L R L R	L R L *
3*5*5*	L R L *	L R L R	L * L R	L R L *
7*7*	L R L R	L R L *	L R L R	L R L *
3*1*3*1*3*	L R L *	L * L R	L * L *	L R L *
5*1*5*1*	L R L R	L * L *	L R L R	L * L *
3*5*1*3*	L R L *	L R L R	L * L *	L R L *
3*1*7*1*	L R L *	L * L R	L R L R	L * L *
3*1*1*5*1*	L R L *	L * L *	L R L R	L * L *
7*1*5*	L R L R	L R L *	L * L R	L R L *

ACCENT VARIATIONS

LESSON ONE
BASIC PATTERN ACCENTS

BASIC PATTERNS
RIGHT HAND
REVERSE ACCENTS- FIRST NOTE

3*3*3*3*	**R** L R *	**R** L R *	**R** L R *	**R** L R *
3*3*7*	**R** L R *	**R** L R *	**R** L R L	R L R *
3*5*5*	**R** L R *	**R** L R L	R * **R** L	R L R *
7*7*	**R** L R L	R L R *	**R** L R L	R L R *
3*1*3*1*3*	**R** L R *	**R** * **R** L	R * **R** *	**R** L R *
5*1*5*1*	**R** L R L	R * **R** *	**R** L R L	R * **R** *
3*5*1*3*	**R** L R *	**R** L R L	R * **R** *	**R** L R *
3*1*7*1*	**R** L R *	**R** * **R** L	R L R L	R * **R** *
3*1*1*5*1*	**R** L R *	**R** * R *	**R** L R L	R * **R** *
7*1*5*	**R** L R L	R L R *	**R** * **R** L	R L R *

ACCENT VARIATIONS

LESSON ONE
BASIC PATTERN ACCENTS

BASIC PATTERNS
LEFT HAND
REVERSE ACCENTS- FIRST NOTE

3*3*3*3*	L R L *	L R L *	L R L *	L R L *
3*3*7*	L R L *	L R L *	L R L R	L R L *
3*5*5*	L R L *	L R L R	L * L R	L R L *
7*7*	L R L R	L R L *	L R L R	L R L *
3*1*3*1*3*	L R L *	L * L R	L * L *	L R L *
5*1*5*1*	L R L R	L * L *	L R L R	L * L *
3*5*1*3*	L R L *	L R L R	L * L *	L R L *
3*1*7*1*	L R L *	L * L R	L R L R	L * L *
3*1*1*5*1*	L R L *	L * L *	L R L R	L * L *
7*1*5*	L R L R	L R L *	L * L R	L R L *

ACCENT VARIATIONS

LESSON ONE
BASIC PATTERN ACCENTS

BASIC PATTERNS
RIGHT HAND
CENTER ACCENTS- MIDDLE NOTE

3*3*3*3*	R _L_ R *	R _L_ R *	R _L_ R *	R _L_ R *
3*3*7*	R _L_ R *	R _L_ R *	R L R _L_	R _L_ R *
3*5*5*	R _L_ R *	R L _R_ L	R * R L	_R_ L R *
7*7*	R L R _L_	R L R *	R L R _L_	R L R *
3*1*3*1*3*	R _L_ R *	_R_ * R L	R * _R_ *	R _L_ R *
5*1*5*1*	R L _R_ L	R * _R_ *	R L _R_ L	R * _R_ *
3*5*1*3*	R _L_ R *	R L _R_ L	R * _R_ *	R _L_ R *
3*1*7*1*	R _L_ R *	_R_ * R L	R _L_ R L	R * _R_ *
3*1*1*5*1*	R _L_ R *	_R_ * R *	R L _R_ L	R * _R_ *
7*1*5*	R L R _L_	R L R *	_R_ * R L	_R_ L R *

RHYTHM FACTORING

ACCENT VARIATIONS

LESSON ONE
BASIC PATTERN ACCENTS

BASIC PATTERNS
LEFT HAND
CENTER ACCENTS- MIDDLE NOTE

3*3*3*3*	L <u>R</u> L *	L <u>R</u> L *	L <u>R</u> L *	L <u>R</u> L *
3*3*7*	L <u>R</u> L *	L <u>R</u> L *	L R L <u>R</u>	L R L *
3*5*5*	L <u>R</u> L *	L R <u>L</u> R	L * L R	<u>L</u> R L *
7*7*	L R L <u>R</u>	L R L *	L R L <u>R</u>	L R L *
3*1*3*1*3*	L <u>R</u> L *	<u>L</u> * L <u>R</u>	L * <u>L</u> *	L <u>R</u> L *
5*1*5*1*	L R <u>L</u> R	L * <u>L</u> *	L R <u>L</u> R	L * <u>L</u> *
3*5*1*3*	L <u>R</u> L *	L R <u>L</u> R	L * <u>L</u> *	L <u>R</u> L *
3*1*7*1*	L <u>R</u> L *	<u>L</u> * L R	L <u>R</u> L R	L * <u>L</u> *
3*1*1*5*1*	L <u>R</u> L *	<u>L</u> * <u>L</u> *	L R L <u>R</u>	L * <u>L</u> *
7*1*5*	L R L <u>R</u>	L R L *	<u>L</u> * L R	<u>L</u> R L *

ACCENT VARIATIONS

LESSON TWO
STANDARD ACCENT TABLES RIGHT AND LEFT

3-3-7 RIGHT HAND
STANDARD ACCENTS- END NOTE

3*3*7*	R L <u>R</u> *	R L <u>R</u> *	R L R L	R L <u>R</u> *
3*7*3*	R L <u>R</u> *	R L R L	R L <u>R</u> *	R L <u>R</u> *
7*3*3*	R L R L	R L <u>R</u> *	R L <u>R</u> *	R L <u>R</u> *

3-3-7 LEFT HAND
STANDARD ACCENTS- END NOTE

3*3*7*	L R <u>L</u> *	L R <u>L</u> *	L R L R	L R <u>L</u> *
3*7*3*	L R <u>L</u> *	L R L R	L R <u>L</u> *	L R <u>L</u> *
7*3*3*	L R L R	L R <u>L</u> *	L R <u>L</u> *	L R <u>L</u> *

3-5-5 RIGHT HAND
STANDARD ACCENT- END NOTE

3*5*5*	R L <u>R</u> *	R L R L	<u>R</u> * R L	R L <u>R</u> *
5*3*5*	R L R L	<u>R</u> * R L	<u>R</u> * R L	R L <u>R</u> *
5*5*3*	R L R L	<u>R</u> * R L	R L <u>R</u> *	R L <u>R</u> *

3-5-5 LEFT HAND
STANDARD ACCENT- END NOTE

3*5*5*	L R <u>L</u> *	L R L R	<u>L</u> * L R	L R <u>L</u> *
5*3*5*	L R L R	<u>L</u> * L R	<u>L</u> * L R	L R <u>L</u> *
5*5*3*	L R L R	<u>L</u> * L R	L R <u>L</u> *	L R <u>L</u> *

ACCENT VARIATIONS

LESSON TWO
STANDARD ACCENT TABLES RIGHT AND LEFT

3-1-3-1-3 RIGHT HAND
STANDARD ACCENTS END NOTE

3*1*3*1*3*	R L R *	R * R L	R * R *	R L R *
1*3*3*1*3*	R * R L	R * R L	R * R *	R L R *
1*3*1*3*3*	R * R L	R * R *	R L R *	R L R *
3*3*1*3*1*	R L R *	R L R *	R * R L	R * R *
3*1*3*3*1*	R L R *	R * R L	R * R L	R * R *
1*1*3*3*3*	R * R *	R L R *	R L R *	R L R *
3*1*1*3*3*	R L R *	R * R *	R L R *	R L R *
3*3*1*1*3*	R L R *	R L R *	R * R *	R L R *

3-1-3-1-3 LEFT HAND
STANDARD ACCENT- END NOTE

3*1*3*1*3*	L R L *	L * L R	L * L *	L R L *
1*3*3*1*3*	L * L R	L * L R	L * L *	L R L *
1*3*1*3*3*	L * L R	L * L *	L R L *	L R L *
3*3*1*3*1*	L R L *	L R L *	L * L R	L * L *
3*1*3*3*1*	L R L *	L * L R	L * L R	L * L *
1*1*3*3*3*	L * L *	L R L *	L R L *	L R L *
3*1*1*3*3*	L R L *	L * L *	L R L *	L R L *
3*3*1*1*3*	L R L *	L R L *	L * L *	L R L *

ACCENT VARIATIONS

LESSON TWO
STANDARD ACCENT TABLES RIGHT AND LEFT

5-1-5-1 RIGHT HAND
STANDARD ACCENT- END NOTE

5*1*5*1*	R L R L	R * R *	R L R L	R * R *
5*1*1*5*	R L R L	R * R *	R * R L	R L R *
5*5*1*1*	R L R L	R * R L	R L R *	R * R *
1*1*5*5*	R * R *	R L R L	R * R L	R L R *
1*5*1*5*	R * R L	R L R *	R * R L	R L R *
1*5*5*1*	R * R L	R L R *	R L R L	R * R *

5-1-5-1 LEFT HAND
STANDARD ACCENT- END NOTE

5*1*5*1*	L R L R	L * L *	L R L R	L * L *
5*1*1*5*	L R L R	L * L *	L * L R	L R L *
5*5*1*1*	L R L R	L * L R	L R L *	L * L *
1*1*5*5*	L * L *	L R L R	L * L R	L R L *
1*5*1*5*	L * L R	L R L *	L * L R	L R L *
1*5*5*1*	L * L R	L R L *	L R L R	L * L *

ACCENT VARIATIONS

LESSON TWO
STANDARD ACCENT TABLES RIGHT AND LEFT

3-5-1-3 RIGHT HAND
STANDARD ACCENT- END NOTE

3*5*1*3*	R L <u>R</u> *	R L R L	<u>R</u> * <u>R</u> *	R L <u>R</u> *
5*1*3*3*	R L R L	<u>R</u> * <u>R</u> *	R L <u>R</u> *	R L <u>R</u> *
1*3*3*5*	<u>R</u> * R L	<u>R</u> * R L	<u>R</u> * R L	R L <u>R</u> *
1*3*5*3*	<u>R</u> * R L	<u>R</u> * R L	R L <u>R</u> *	R L <u>R</u> *
1*5*3*3*	<u>R</u> * R L	R L <u>R</u> *	R L <u>R</u> *	R L <u>R</u> *
5*3*3*1*	R L R L	<u>R</u> * R L	<u>R</u> * R L	<u>R</u> * <u>R</u> *
5*3*1*3*	R L R L	<u>R</u> * R L	<u>R</u> * <u>R</u> *	R L <u>R</u> *
3*1*5*3*	R L <u>R</u> *	<u>R</u> * R L	R L <u>R</u> *	R L <u>R</u> *

3-5-1-3 LEFT HAND
STANDARD ACCENT- END NOTE

3*5*1*3*	L R <u>L</u> *	L R L R	<u>L</u> * <u>L</u> *	L R <u>L</u> *
5*1*3*3*	L R L R	<u>L</u> * <u>L</u> *	L R <u>L</u> *	L R <u>L</u> *
1*3*3*5*	<u>L</u> * L R	<u>L</u> * L R	<u>L</u> * L R	L R <u>L</u> *
1*3*5*3*	<u>L</u> * L R	<u>L</u> * L R	L R <u>L</u> *	L R <u>L</u> *
1*5*3*3*	<u>L</u> * L R	L R <u>L</u> *	L R <u>L</u> *	L R <u>L</u> *
5*3*3*1*	L R L R	<u>L</u> * L R	<u>L</u> * L R	<u>L</u> * <u>L</u> *
5*3*1*3*	L R L R	<u>L</u> * L R	<u>L</u> * <u>L</u> *	L R <u>L</u> *
3*1*5*3*	L R <u>L</u> *	<u>L</u> * L R	L R <u>L</u> *	L R <u>L</u> *

ACCENT VARIATIONS

LESSON TWO
STANDARD ACCENT TABLES RIGHT AND LEFT

7-1-5 RIGHT HAND
STANDARD ACCENT- END NOTE

7*1*5*	R L R L	R L R *	R * R L	R L R *
7*5*1*	R L R L	R L R *	R L R L	R * R *
5*7*1*	R L R L	R * R L	R L R L	R * R *
5*1*7*	R L R L	R * R *	R L R L	R L R *
1*7*5*	R * R L	R L R L	R * R L	R L R *
1*5*7*	R * R L	R L R *	R L R L	R L R *

7-1-5 LEFT HAND
STANDARD ACCENT- END NOTE

7*1*5*	L R L R	L R L *	L * L R	L R L *
7*5*1*	L R L R	L R L *	L R L R	L * L *
5*7*1*	L R L R	L * L R	L R L R	L * L *
5*1*7*	L R L R	L * L *	L R L R	L R L *
1*7*5*	L * L R	L R L R	L * L R	L R L *
1*5*7*	L * L R	L R L *	L R L R	L R L *

ACCENT VARIATIONS

LESSON TWO
STANDARD ACCENT TABLES RIGHT AND LEFT

3-1-1-5-1 RIGHT HAND
STANDARD ACCENT- END NOTE

3*1*1*5*1*	R L R *	R * R *	R L R L	R * R *
3*1*1*1*5*	R L R *	R * R *	R * R L	R L R *
3*1*5*1*1*	R L R *	R * R L	R L R *	R * R *
3*5*1*1*1*	R L R *	R L R L	R * R *	R * R *
5*3*1*1*1*	R L R L	R * R L	R * R *	R * R *
5*1*1*1*3*	R L R L	R * R *	R * R *	R L R *
5*1*1*3*1*	R L R L	R * R *	R * R L	R * R *
5*1*3*1*1*	R L R L	R * R *	R L R *	R * R *

3-1-1-5-1 LEFT HAND
STANDARD ACCENT- END NOTE

3*1*1*5*1*	L R L *	L * L *	L R L R	L * L *
3*1*1*1*5*	L R L *	L * L *	L * L R	L R L *
3*1*5*1*1*	L R L *	L * L R	L R L *	L * L *
3*5*1*1*1*	L R L *	L R L R	L * L *	L * L *
5*3*1*1*1*	L R L R	L * L R	L * L *	L * L *
5*1*1*1*3*	L R L R	L * L *	L * L *	L R L *
5*1*1*3*1*	L R L R	L * L *	L * L R	L * L *
5*1*3*1*1*	L R L R	L * L *	L R L *	L * L *

ACCENT VARIATIONS

LESSON TWO
STANDARD ACCENT TABLES RIGHT AND LEFT

3-1-7-1 RIGHT HAND
STANDARD ACCENT- END NOTE

3*1*7*1*	R L **R** *	**R** * R L	R L R L	**R** * **R** *
3*1*1*7*	R L **R** *	**R** * **R** *	R L R L	R L **R** *
3*7*1*1*	R L **R** *	R L R L	R L **R** *	**R** * **R** *
7*1*1*3*	R L R L	R L **R** *	**R** * **R** *	R L **R** *
7*1*3*1*	R L R L	R L **R** *	**R** * R L	**R** * **R** *
7*3*1*1*	R L R L	R L **R** *	R L **R** *	**R** * **R** *
1*3*7*1*	**R** * R L	**R** * R L	R L R L	**R** * **R** *
1*3*1*7*	**R** * R L	**R** * **R** *	R L R L	R L **R** *

3-1-7-1- LEFT HAND
STANDARD ACCENT- END NOTE

3*1*7*1*	L R **L** *	**L** * L R	L R L R	**L** * **L** *
3*1*1*7*	L R **L** *	**L** * **L** *	L R L R	L R **L** *
3*7*1*1*	L R **L** *	L R L R	L R **L** *	**L** * **L** *
7*1*1*3*	L R L R	L R **L** *	**L** * **L** *	L R **L** *
7*1*3*1*	L R L R	L R **L** *	**L** * L R	**L** * **L** *
7*3*1*1*	L R L R	L R **L** *	L R **L** *	**L** * **L** *
1*3*7*1*	**L** * L R	**L** * L R	L R L R	**L** * **L** *
1*3*1*7*	**L** * L R	**L** * **L** *	L R L R	L R **L** *

ACCENT VARIATIONS

LESSON TWO
STANDARD ACCENT TABLES RIGHT AND LEFT

1-3-1-1-1-3 RIGHT HAND
STANDARD ACCENTS- END NOTE

1*3*1*1*1*3	<u>R</u> * R L	<u>R</u> * <u>R</u> *	<u>R</u> * <u>R</u> *	R L <u>R</u> *
1*1*1*3*1*3	<u>R</u> * <u>R</u> *	<u>R</u> * R L	<u>R</u> * <u>R</u> *	R L <u>R</u> *
1*1*1*3*3*1	<u>R</u> * <u>R</u> *	<u>R</u> * R L	<u>R</u> * R L	<u>R</u> * <u>R</u> *
1*1*1*1*3*3	<u>R</u> * <u>R</u> *	<u>R</u> * <u>R</u> *	R L <u>R</u> *	R L <u>R</u> *
1*1*3*3*1*1	<u>R</u> * <u>R</u> *	R L <u>R</u> *	R L <u>R</u> *	<u>R</u> * <u>R</u> *
1*1*3*1*3*1	<u>R</u> * <u>R</u> *	R L <u>R</u> *	<u>R</u> * R L	<u>R</u> * <u>R</u> *
1*1*3*1*1*3	<u>R</u> * <u>R</u> *	R L <u>R</u> *	<u>R</u> * <u>R</u> *	R L <u>R</u> *

1-3-1-1-1-3 LEFT HAND
STANDARD ACCENT- END NOTE

1*3*1*1*1*3	<u>L</u> * L R	<u>L</u> * <u>L</u> *	<u>L</u> * <u>L</u> *	L R <u>L</u> *
1*1*1*3*1*3	<u>L</u> * <u>L</u> *	<u>L</u> * L R	<u>L</u> * <u>L</u> *	L R <u>L</u> *
1*1*1*3*3*1	<u>L</u> * <u>L</u> *	<u>L</u> * L R	<u>L</u> * L R	<u>L</u> * <u>L</u> *
1*1*1*1*3*3	<u>L</u> * <u>L</u> *	<u>L</u> * <u>L</u> *	L R <u>L</u> *	L R <u>L</u> *
1*1*3*3*1*1	<u>L</u> * <u>L</u> *	L R <u>L</u> *	L R <u>L</u> *	<u>L</u> * <u>L</u> *
1*1*3*1*3*1	<u>L</u> * <u>L</u> *	L R <u>L</u> *	<u>L</u> * L R	<u>L</u> * <u>L</u> *
1*1*3*1*1*3	<u>L</u> * <u>L</u> *	L R <u>L</u> *	<u>L</u> * <u>L</u> *	L R <u>L</u> *

ACCENT VARIATIONS

LESSON THREE
REVERSE ACCENT TABLES RIGHT AND LEFT

3-3-7 RIGHT HAND
REVERSE ACCENT- FIRST NOTE

3*3*7*	<u>R</u> L R *	<u>R</u> L R *	<u>R</u> L R L	R L R *
3*7*3*	<u>R</u> L R *	<u>R</u> L R L	R L R *	<u>R</u> L R *
7*3*3*	<u>R</u> L R L	R L R *	<u>R</u> L R *	<u>R</u> L R *

3-3–7 LEFT HAND
REVERSE ACCENT- FIRST NOTE

3*3*7*	<u>L</u> R L *	<u>L</u> R L *	<u>L</u> R L R	L R L *
3*7*3*	<u>L</u> R L *	<u>L</u> R L R	L R L *	<u>L</u> R L *
7*3*3*	<u>L</u> R L R	L R L *	<u>L</u> R L *	<u>L</u> R L *

3-5-5 RIGHT HAND
REVERSE ACCENT- FIRST NOTE

3*5*5*	<u>R</u> L R *	<u>R</u> L R L	R * <u>R</u> L	R L R *
5*3*5*	<u>R</u> L R L	R * <u>R</u> L	R * <u>R</u> L	R L R *
5*5*3*	<u>R</u> L R L	R * <u>R</u> L	R L R *	<u>R</u> L R *

3-5-5 LEFT HAND
REVERSE ACCENT- FIRST NOTE

3*5*5*	<u>L</u> R L *	<u>L</u> R L R	L * <u>L</u> R	L R L *
5*3*5*	<u>L</u> R L R	L * <u>L</u> R	L * <u>L</u> R	L R L *
5*5*3*	<u>L</u> R L R	L * <u>L</u> R	L R L *	<u>L</u> R L *

ACCENT VARIATIONS

LESSON THREE
REVERSE ACCENT TABLES RIGHT AND LEFT

3-1-3-1-3 RIGHT HAND
REVERSE ACCENT- FIRST NOTE

3*1*3*1*3*	**R** L R *	**R** * **R** L	R * **R** *	**R** L R *
1*3*3*1*3*	**R** * **R** L	R * **R** L	R * **R** *	**R** L R *
1*3*1*3*3*	**R** * **R** L	R * **R** *	**R** L R *	**R** L R *
3*3*1*3*1*	**R** L R *	**R** L R *	R * **R** L	R * **R** *
3*1*3*3*1*	**R** L R *	R * **R** L	R * **R** L	R * **R** *
1*1*3*3*3*	**R** * **R** *	**R** L R *	**R** L R *	**R** L R *
3*1*1*3*3*	**R** L R *	**R** * **R** *	**R** L R *	**R** L R *
3*3*1*1*3*	**R** L R *	**R** L R *	**R** * **R** *	**R** L R *

3-1-3-1-3 LEFT HAND
REVERSE ACCENT- FIRST NOTE

3*1*3*1*3*	**L** R L *	**L** * **L** R	L * **L** *	**L** R L *
1*3*3*1*3*	**L** * **L** R	L * **L** R	L * **L** *	**L** R L *
1*3*1*3*3*	**L** * **L** R	L * **L** *	**L** R L *	**L** R L *
3*3*1*3*1*	**L** R L *	**L** R L *	**L** * **L** R	L * **L** *
3*1*3*3*1*	**L** R L *	**L** * **L** R	L * **L** R	L * **L** *
1*1*3*3*3*	**L** * **L** *	**L** R L *	**L** R L *	**L** R L *
3*1*1*3*3*	**L** R L *	**L** * **L** *	**L** R L *	**L** R L *
3*3*1*1*3*	**L** R L *	**L** R L *	**L** * **L** *	**L** R L *

ACCENT VARIATIONS

LESSON THREE
REVERSE ACCENT TABLES RIGHT AND LEFT

5-1-5-1 RIGHT HAND
REVERSE ACCENT- FIRST NOTE

5*1*5*1*	R L R L	R * R *	R L R L	R * R *
5*1*1*5*	R L R L	R * R *	R * R L	R L R *
5*5*1*1*	R L R L	R * R L	R L R *	R * R *
1*1*5*5*	R * R *	R L R L	R * R L	R L R *
1*5*1*5*	R * R L	R L R *	R * R L	R L R *
1*5*5*1*	R * R L	R L R *	R L R L	R * R *

5-1-5-1 LEFT HAND
REVERSE ACCENT- FIRST NOTE

5*1*5*1*	L R L R	L * L *	L R L R	L * L *
5*1*1*5*	L R L R	L * L *	L * L R	L R L *
5*5*1*1*	L R L R	L * L R	L R L *	L * L *
1*1*5*5*	L * L *	L R L R	L * L R	L R L *
1*5*1*5*	L * L R	L R L *	L * L R	L R L *
1*5*5*1*	L * L R	L R L *	L R L R	L * L *

ACCENT VARIATIONS

LESSON THREE
REVERSE ACCENT TABLES RIGHT AND LEFT

3-5-1-3 RIGHT HAND
REVERSE ACCENT- FIRST NOTE

3*5*1*3*	**R** L R *	**R** L R L	R * **R** *	**R** L R *
5*1*3*3*	**R** L R L	R * **R** *	**R** L R *	**R** L R *
1*3*3*5*	**R** * R L	R * **R** L	R * **R** L	R L R *
1*3*5*3*	**R** * R L	R * **R** L	R L R *	**R** L R *
1*5*3*3*	**R** * R L	R L R *	**R** L R *	**R** L R *
5*3*3*1*	**R** L R L	R * **R** L	R * **R** L	R * **R** *
5*3*1*3*	**R** L R L	R * **R** L	R * **R** *	**R** L R *
3*1*5*3*	R L R *	R * **R** L	R L R *	**R** L R *

3-5-1-3 LEFT HAND
REVERSE ACCENT- FIRST NOTE

3*5*1*3*	**L** R L *	**L** R L R	L * **L** *	**L** R L *
5*1*3*3*	**L** R L R	L * **L** *	**L** R L *	**L** R L *
1*3*3*5*	**L** * L R	L * **L** R	L * **L** R	L R L *
1*3*5*3*	**L** * L R	L * **L** R	L R L *	**L** R L *
1*5*3*3*	**L** * L R	L R L *	**L** R L *	**L** R L *
5*3*3*1*	**L** R L R	L * **L** R	L * **L** R	L * **L** *
5*3*1*3*	**L** R L R	L * **L** R	L * **L** *	**L** R L *
3*1*5*3*	**L** R L *	L * **L** R	L R L *	**L** R L *

ACCENT VARIATIONS

LESSON THREE
REVERSE ACCENT TABLES RIGHT AND LEFT

7-1-5 RIGHT HAND
REVERSE ACCENT- FIRST NOTE

7*1*5*	<u>R</u> L R L	R L R *	<u>R</u> * <u>R</u> L	R L R *
7*5*1*	<u>R</u> L R L	R L R *	<u>R</u> L R L	R * <u>R</u> *
5*7*1*	<u>R</u> L R L	R * <u>R</u> L	R L R L	R * <u>R</u> *
5*1*7*	<u>R</u> L R L	R * <u>R</u> *	<u>R</u> L R L	R L R *
1*7*5*	<u>R</u> * <u>R</u> L	R L R L	R * <u>R</u> L	R L R *
1*5*7*	<u>R</u> * <u>R</u> L	R L R *	<u>R</u> L R L	R L R *

7-1-5 LEFT HAND
REVERSE ACCENT- FIRST NOTE

7*1*5*	<u>L</u> R L R	L R L *	<u>L</u> * <u>L</u> R	L R L *
7*5*1*	<u>L</u> R L R	L R L *	<u>L</u> R L R	L * <u>L</u> *
5*7*1*	<u>L</u> R L R	L * <u>L</u> R	L R L R	L * <u>L</u> *
5*1*7*	<u>L</u> R L R	L * <u>L</u> *	<u>L</u> R L R	L R L *
1*7*5*	<u>L</u> * <u>L</u> R	L R L R	L * <u>L</u> R	L R L *
1*5*7*	<u>L</u> * <u>L</u> R	L R L *	<u>L</u> R L R	L R L *

ACCENT VARIATIONS

LESSON THREE
REVERSE ACCENT TABLES RIGHT AND LEFT

3-1-1-5-1 RIGHT HAND
REVERSE ACCENT- FIRST NOTE

3*1*1*5*1*	R L R *	R * R *	R L R L	R * R *
3*1*1*1*5*	R L R *	R * R *	R * R L	R L R *
3*1*5*1*1*	R L R *	R * R L	R L R *	R * R *
3*5*1*1*1*	R L R *	R L R L	R * R *	R * R *
5*3*1*1*1*	R L R L	R * R L	R * R *	R * R *
5*1*1*1*3*	R L R L	R * R *	R * R *	R L R *
5*1*1*3*1*	R L R L	R * R *	R * R L	R * R *
5*1*3*1*1*	R L R L	R * R *	R L R *	R * R *

3-1-1-5-1 LEFT HAND
REVERSE ACCENT- FIRST NOTE

3*1*1*5*1*	L R L *	L * L *	L R L R	L * L *
3*1*1*1*5*	L R L *	L * L *	L * L R	L R L *
3*1*5*1*1*	L R L *	L * L R	L R L *	L * L *
3*5*1*1*1*	L R L *	L R L R	L * L *	L * L *
5*3*1*1*1*	L R L R	L * L R	L * L *	L * L *
5*1*1*1*3*	L R L R	L * L *	L * L *	L R L *
5*1*1*3*1*	L R L R	L * L *	L * L R	L * L *
5*1*3*1*1*	L R L R	L * L *	L R L *	L * L *

ACCENT VARIATIONS

LESSON THREE
REVERSE ACCENT TABLES RIGHT AND LEFT

3-1-7-1 RIGHT HAND
REVERSE ACCENT- FIRST NOTE

3*1*7*1*	**R** L R *	**R** * R L	R L R L	R * **R** *
3*1*1*7*	**R** L R *	**R** * R *	**R** L R L	R L R *
3*7*1*1*	**R** L R *	**R** L R L	R L R *	**R** * **R** *
7*1*1*3*	**R** L R L	R L R *	R * **R** *	**R** L R *
7*1*3*1*	**R** L R L	R L R *	R * **R** L	R * **R** *
7*3*1*1*	**R** L R L	R L R *	**R** L R *	**R** * **R** *
1*3*7*1*	R * **R** L	R * **R** L	R L R L	R * **R** *
1*3*1*7*	R * **R** L	R * **R** *	**R** L R L	R L R *

3-1-7-1 LEFT HAND
REVERSE ACCENT- FIRST NOTE

3*1*7*1*	**L** R L *	**L** * **L** R	L R L R	L * **L** *
3*1*1*7*	**L** R L *	**L** * L *	**L** R L R	L R L *
3*7*1*1*	**L** R L *	**L** R L R	L R L *	**L** * **L** *
7*1*1*3*	**L** R L R	L R L *	**L** * L *	**L** R L *
7*1*3*1*	**L** R L R	L R L *	**L** * L R	L * **L** *
7*3*1*1*	**L** R L R	L R L *	**L** R L *	**L** * **L** *
1*3*7*1*	**L** * **L** R	L * **L** R	L R L R	L * **L** *
1*3*1*7*	**L** * **L** R	L * **L** *	**L** R L R	L R L *

ACCENT VARIATIONS

LESSON THREE
REVERSE ACCENT TABLES RIGHT AND LEFT

1-3-1-1-1-3 RIGHT HAND
REVERSE ACCENT- FIRST NOTE

1*3*1*1*1*3	_R_ * _R_ L	R * _R_ *	_R_ * _R_ *	_R_ L R *
1*1*1*3*1*3	_R_ * _R_ *	_R_ * _R_ L	R * _R_ *	_R_ L R *
1*1*1*3*3*1	_R_ * _R_ *	_R_ * _R_ L	R * _R_ L	R * _R_ *
1*1*1*1*3*3	_R_ * _R_ *	_R_ * _R_ *	_R_ L R *	_R_ L R *
1*1*3*3*1*1	_R_ * _R_ *	_R_ L R *	_R_ L R *	_R_ * _R_ *
1*1*3*1*3*1	_R_ * _R_ *	_R_ L R *	R * _R_ L	R * _R_ *
1*1*3*1*1*3	_R_ * _R_ *	_R_ L R *	_R_ * _R_ *	_R_ L R *

1-3-1-1-1-3 LEFT HAND
REVERSE ACCENT- FIRST NOTE

1*3*1*1*1*3	_L_ * _L_ R	L * _L_ *	_L_ * _L_ *	_L_ R L *
1*1*1*3*1*3	_L_ * _L_ *	_L_ * _L_ R	L * _L_ *	_L_ R L *
1*1*1*3*3*1	_L_ * _L_ *	_L_ * _L_ R	L * _L_ R	L * _L_ *
1*1*1*1*3*3	_L_ * _L_ *	_L_ * _L_ *	_L_ R L *	_L_ R L *
1*1*3*3*1*1	_L_ * _L_ *	_L_ R L *	_L_ R L *	_L_ * _L_ *
1*1*3*1*3*1	_L_ * _L_ *	_L_ R L *	_L_ * _L_ R	L * _L_ *
1*1*3*1*1*3	_L_ * _L_ *	_L_ R L *	_L_ * _L_ *	_L_ R L *

ACCENT VARIATIONS

LESSON FOUR
CENTER ACCENT TABLES RIGHT AND LEFT

3-3-7 RIGHT HAND
CENTER ACCENT- MIDDLE NOTE

3*3*7*	R **L** R *	R **L** R *	R L R **L**	R **L** R *
3*7*3*	R **L** R *	R L R **L**	R **L** R *	R **L** R *
7*3*3*	R L R **L**	R **L** R *	R **L** R *	R **L** R *

3-3-7 LEFT HAND
CENTER ACCENT- MIDDLE NOTE

3*3*7*	L **R** L *	L **R** L *	L R L **R**	L **R** L *
3*7*3*	L **R** L *	L R L **R**	L **R** L *	L **R** L *
7*3*3*	L R L **R**	L **R** L *	L **R** L *	L **R** L *

3-5-5 RIGHT HAND
CENTER ACCENT- MIDDLE NOTE

3*5*5*	R **L** R *	R L **R** L	R * R L	**R** L R *
5*3*5*	R L **R** L	R * R L	R * R L	**R** L R *
5*5*3*	R L **R** L	R * R L	**R** L R *	R **L** R *

3-5-5 LEFT HAND
CENTER ACCENT- MIDDLE NOTE

3*5*5*	L **R** L *	L R **L** R	L * L R	**L** R L *
5*3*5*	L R **L** R	L * L R	L * L R	**L** R L *
5*5*3*	L R **L** R	L * L R	**L** R L *	L **R** L *

ACCENT VARIATIONS

LESSON FOUR
CENTER ACCENT TABLES RIGHT AND LEFT

3-1-3-1-3 RIGHT HAND
CENTER ACCENT- MIDDLE NOTE

3*1*3*1*3*	R <u>L</u> R *	<u>R</u> * R <u>L</u>	R * <u>R</u> *	R <u>L</u> R *
1*3*3*1*3*	<u>R</u> * R L	R * R <u>L</u>	R * <u>R</u> *	R <u>L</u> R *
1*3*1*3*3*	<u>R</u> * R L	R * <u>R</u> *	R <u>L</u> R *	R <u>L</u> R *
3*3*1*3*1*	R <u>L</u> R *	R <u>L</u> R *	<u>R</u> * R <u>L</u>	R * <u>R</u> *
3*1*3*3*1*	R <u>L</u> R *	<u>R</u> * R L	R * R <u>L</u>	R * <u>R</u> *
1*1*3*3*3*	<u>R</u> * <u>R</u> *	R <u>L</u> R *	R <u>L</u> R *	R <u>L</u> R *
3*1*1*3*3*	R <u>L</u> R *	<u>R</u> * <u>R</u> *	R <u>L</u> R *	R <u>L</u> R *
3*3*1*1*3*	R <u>L</u> R *	R <u>L</u> R *	<u>R</u> * <u>R</u> *	R <u>L</u> R *

3-1-3-1-3 LEFT HAND
CENTER ACCENT- MIDDLE NOTE

3*1*3*1*3*	L <u>R</u> L *	<u>L</u> * L <u>R</u>	L * <u>L</u> *	L <u>R</u> L *
1*3*3*1*3*	<u>L</u> * L <u>R</u>	L * L <u>R</u>	L * <u>L</u> *	L <u>R</u> L *
1*3*1*3*3*	<u>L</u> * L <u>R</u>	L * <u>L</u> *	L <u>R</u> L *	L <u>R</u> L *
3*3*1*3*1*	L <u>R</u> L *	L <u>R</u> L *	<u>L</u> * L <u>R</u>	L * <u>L</u> *
3*1*3*3*1*	L <u>R</u> L *	<u>L</u> * L <u>R</u>	L * L <u>R</u>	L * <u>L</u> *
1*1*3*3*3*	<u>L</u> * <u>L</u> *	L <u>R</u> L *	L <u>R</u> L *	L <u>R</u> L *
3*1*1*3*3*	L <u>R</u> L *	<u>L</u> * <u>L</u> *	L <u>R</u> L *	L <u>R</u> L *
3*3*1*1*3*	L <u>R</u> L *	L <u>R</u> L *	<u>L</u> * <u>L</u> *	L <u>R</u> L *

ACCENT VARIATIONS

LESSON FOUR
CENTER ACCENT TABLES RIGHT AND LEFT

5-1-5-1 RIGHT HAND
CENTER ACCENTS- MIDDLE NOTE

5*1*5*1*	R L <u>R</u> L	R * <u>R</u> *	R L <u>R</u> L	R * <u>R</u> *
5*1*1*5*	R L R L	<u>R</u> * <u>R</u> *	<u>R</u> * R L	<u>R</u> L R *
5*5*1*1*	R L R L	R * R L	<u>R</u> L R *	<u>R</u> * <u>R</u> *
1*1*5*5*	<u>R</u> * <u>R</u> *	R L <u>R</u> L	R * R L	<u>R</u> L R *
1*5*1*5*	<u>R</u> * R L	<u>R</u> L R *	<u>R</u> * R L	<u>R</u> L R *
1*5*5*1*	<u>R</u> * R L	<u>R</u> L R *	R L <u>R</u> L	R * <u>R</u> *

5-1-5-1 LEFT HAND
CENTER ACCENT- MIDDLE NOTE

5*1*5*1*	L R <u>L</u> R	L * <u>L</u> *	L R <u>L</u> R	L * <u>L</u> *
5*1*1*5*	L R <u>L</u> R	L * <u>L</u> *	<u>L</u> * L R	<u>L</u> R L *
5*5*1*1*	L R <u>L</u> R	L * L R	<u>L</u> R L *	<u>L</u> * <u>L</u> *
1*1*5*5*	<u>L</u> * <u>L</u> *	L R <u>L</u> R	L * L R	<u>L</u> R L *
1*5*1*5*	<u>L</u> * L R	<u>L</u> R L *	<u>L</u> * L R	<u>L</u> R L *
1*5*5*1*	<u>L</u> * L R	<u>L</u> R L *	L R <u>L</u> R	L * <u>L</u> *

ACCENT VARIATIONS

LESSON FOUR
CENTER ACCENT TABLES RIGHT AND LEFT

3-5-1-3 RIGHT HAND
CENTER ACCENT- MIDDLE NOTE

3*5*1*3*	R **L** R *	R L **R** L	R * **R** *	R **L** R *
5*1*3*3*	R L **R** L	R * **R** *	R **L** R *	R **L** R *
1*3*3*5*	**R** * R **L**	R * R **L**	R * R **L**	**R** L R *
1*3*5*3*	**R** * R **L**	R * R **L**	**R** L R *	R **L** R *
1*5*3*3*	**R** * R L	**R** L R *	R **L** R *	R **L** R *
5*3*3*1*	R L **R** L	R * R **L**	R * R **L**	R * **R** *
5*3*1*3*	R L **R** L	R * R **L**	R * **R** *	R **L** R *
3*1*5*3*	R **L** R *	**R** * R L	**R** L R *	R **L** R *

3-5-1-3 LEFT HAND
CENTER ACCENT- MIDDLE NOTE

3*5*1*3*	L **R** L *	L R **L** R	L * **L** *	L **R** L *
5*1*3*3*	L R **L** R	L * **L** *	L **R** L *	L **R** L *
1*3*3*5*	**L** * L **R**	L * L **R**	L * L **R**	**L** R L *
1*3*5*3*	**L** * L **R**	L * L R	**L** R L *	L **R** L *
1*5*3*3*	**L** * L R	**L** R L *	L **R** L *	L **R** L *
5*3*3*1*	L R **L** R	L * L **R**	L * L **R**	L * **L** *
5*3*1*3*	L R **L** R	L * L **R**	L * **L** *	L **R** L *
3*1*5*3*	L **R** L *	**L** * L R	**L** R L *	L **R** L *

ACCENT VARIATIONS

LESSON FOUR
CENTER ACCENT TABLES RIGHT AND LEFT

7-1-5 RIGHT HAND
CENTER ACCENT- MIDDLE NOTE

7*1*5*	R L R <u>L</u>	R L R *	<u>R</u> * R L	<u>R</u> L R *
7*5*1*	R L R <u>L</u>	R L R *	R L <u>R</u> L	R * <u>R</u> *
5*7*1*	R L <u>R</u> L	R * R L	R <u>L</u> R L	R * <u>R</u> *
5*1*7*	R L <u>R</u> L	R * <u>R</u> *	R L R <u>L</u>	R L R *
1*7*5*	<u>R</u> * R L	R <u>L</u> R L	R * R L	<u>R</u> L R *
1*5*7*	<u>R</u> * R L	<u>R</u> L R *	R L R <u>L</u>	R L R *

7-1-5 LEFT HAND
CENTER ACCENT- MIDDLE NOTE

7*1*5*	L R L <u>R</u>	L R L *	<u>L</u> * L R	<u>L</u> R L *
7*5*1*	L R L <u>R</u>	L R L *	L R <u>L</u> R	L * <u>L</u> *
5*7*1*	L R <u>L</u> R	L * L R	L <u>R</u> L R	L * <u>L</u> *
5*1*7*	L R <u>L</u> R	L * <u>L</u> *	L R L <u>R</u>	L R L *
1*7*5*	<u>L</u> * L R	L <u>R</u> L R	L * L R	<u>L</u> R L *
1*5*7*	<u>L</u> * L R	<u>L</u> R L *	L R L <u>R</u>	L R L *

ACCENT VARIATIONS

LESSON FOUR
CENTER ACCENT TABLES RIGHT AND LEFT

3-1-1-5-1 RIGHT HAND
CENTER ACCENT- MIDDLE NOTE

3*1*1*5*1*	R _L_ R *	_R_ * _R_ *	R L _R_ L	R * _R_ *
3*1*1*1*5*	R _L_ R *	_R_ * _R_ *	_R_ * R L	R L R *
3*1*5*1*1*	R _L_ R *	_R_ * R L	_R_ L R *	_R_ * _R_ *
3*5*1*1*1*	R _L_ R *	R L _R_ L	R * _R_ *	_R_ * _R_ *
5*3*1*1*1*	R L _R_ L	R * R _L_	R * _R_ *	_R_ * _R_ *
5*1*1*1*3*	R L _R_ L	R * _R_ *	_R_ * _R_ *	R _L_ R *
5*1*1*3*1*	R L _R_ L	R * _R_ *	_R_ * R _L_	R * _R_ *
5*1*3*1*1*	R L _R_ L	R * _R_ *	R _L_ R *	_R_ * _R_ *

3-1-1-5-1 LEFT HAND
CENTER ACCENT- MIDDLE NOTE

3*1*1*5*1*	L _R_ L *	_L_ * _L_ *	L R _L_ R	L * _L_ *
3*1*1*1*5*	L _R_ L *	_L_ * _L_ *	_L_ * L R	_L_ R L *
3*1*5*1*1*	L _R_ L *	_L_ * L R	_L_ R L *	_L_ * _L_ *
3*5*1*1*1*	L _R_ L *	L R _L_ R	L * _L_ *	_L_ * _L_ *
5*3*1*1*1*	L R _L_ R	L * L _R_	L * _L_ *	_L_ * _L_ *
5*1*1*1*3*	L R _L_ R	L * _L_ *	_L_ * _L_ *	L _R_ L *
5*1*1*3*1*	L R _L_ R	L * _L_ *	_L_ * L _R_	L * _L_ *
5*1*3*1*1*	L R _L_ R	L * _L_ *	L _R_ L *	_L_ * _L_ *

ACCENT VARIATIONS

LESSON FOUR
CENTER ACCENT TABLES RIGHT AND LEFT

3-1-7-1 RIGHT HAND
CENTER ACCENT- MIDDLE NOTE

3*1*7*1*	R L R *	R * R L	R L R L	R * R *
3*1*1*7*	R L R *	R * R *	R L R L	R L R *
3*7*1*1*	R L R *	R L R L	R L R *	R * R *
7*1*1*3*	R L R L	R L R *	R * R *	R L R *
7*1*3*1*	R L R L	R L R *	R * R L	R * R *
7*3*1*1*	R L R L	R L R *	R L R *	R * R *
1*3*7*1*	R * R L	R * R L	R L R L	R * R *
1*3*1*7*	R * R L	R * R *	R L R L	R L R *

3-1-7-1- LEFT HAND
CENTER ACCENT- MIDDLE NOTE

3*1*7*1*	L R L *	L * L R	L R L R	L * L *
3*1*1*7*	L R L *	L * L *	L R L R	L R L *
3*7*1*1*	L R L *	L R L R	L R L *	L * L *
7*1*1*3*	L R L R	L R L *	L * L *	L R L *
7*1*3*1*	L R L R	L R L *	L * L R	L * L *
7*3*1*1*	L R L R	L R L *	L R L *	L * L *
1*3*7*1*	L * L R	L * L R	L R L R	L * L *
1*3*1*7*	L * L R	L * L *	L R L R	L R L *

ACCENT VARIATIONS

LESSON FOUR
CENTER ACCENT TABLES RIGHT AND LEFT

1-3-1-1-1-3 RIGHT HAND
CENTER ACCENT- MIDDLE NOTE

1*3*1*1*1*3	R * R L	R * R *	R * R *	R L R *
1*1*1*3*1*3	R * R *	R * R L	R * R *	R L R *
1*1*1*3*3*1	R * R *	R * R L	R * R L	R * R *
1*1*1*1*3*3	R * R *	R * R *	R L R *	R L R *
1*1*3*3*1*1	R * R *	R L R *	R L R *	R * R *
1*1*3*1*3*1	R * R *	R L R *	R * R L	R * R *
1*1*3*1*1*3	R * R *	R L R *	R * R *	R L R *

1-3-1-1-1-3 LEFT HAND
CENTER ACCENT- MIDDLE NOTE

1*3*1*1*1*3	L * L R	L * L *	L * L *	L R L *
1*1*1*3*1*3	L * L *	L * L R	L * L *	L R L *
1*1*1*3*3*1	L * L *	L * L R	L * L R	L * L *
1*1*1*1*3*3	L * L *	L * L *	L R L *	L R L *
1*1*3*3*1*1	L * L *	L R L *	L R L *	L * L *
1*1*3*1*3*1	L * L *	L R L *	L * L R	L * L *
1*1*3*1*1*3	L * L *	L R L *	L * L *	L R L *

SECTION 3

HAND DRUM NOTATION

HAND DRUM NOTATION

INTRODUCTION TO HAND DRUMMING NOTATION

Any pattern from the Rhythm Factoring method can be played with a variety of types of hand drums and percussive instruments using this simple 3-note translation.

COMMON HAND DRUMS

There are many types of hand drums. Some are small and held on the lap, others require a strap around the neck. Some are played with sticks. Some are played while marching, others are played sitting down. Frame drums are held at the chest supported by one, giving the other hand more movement option. Musicians with great skill, may add complexity and additional notes, but for the purposes of this method, we are focusing on simple patterns with a relatively slow pace, played with open hands.

FACTORING DRUM NOTATION

Drum notation works very well with rhythm factoring. Simply replace all DOOM and TEK (TEK) notes with right hand notation, underlining all the DOOM spots. Then replace all KA notes with left hand notation. This process will instantly convert any drum notation song into a format that can be played according to the Rhythm Factoring method.

COMMON DRUM NOTES- DOOM TEK KA

The basic three notes of hand drumming notation are played with open palm on the drum surface. These common names are used in multiple musical traditions.

DOOM- The first note- DOOM is played with the right hand in the center of the drum and represents the accented note of a rhythm pattern. DOOM notes can also be played by the left hand, but typically this would only happen if the drummer were left hand dominant.

TEK- The second note TEK is played by the right hand, but on the rim of the drum. TEK notes can also be played by the left hand, but typically this would only happen if the drummer were left hand dominant.

KA- The third note KA is played by the left hand, also on the rim of the drum. KA notes can also be played by the right hand, but typically this would only happen if the drummer were left hand dominant.

HAND DRUM NOTATION

SECTION 1 BASIC FACTOR PATTERNS
LESSON ONE
INTRODUCING BASIC PATTERNS

RIGHT HAND BASIC DRUM PATTERNS

3*3*3*3*	Tek Ka Doom *	Tek Ka Doom *	Tek Ka Doom *	Tek Ka Doom *

7*7*	Tek Ka Tek Ka	Tek Ka Doom *	Tek Ka Tek Ka	Tek Ka Doom *

3*3*7*	Tek Ka Doom *	Tek Ka Doom *	Tek Ka Tek Ka	Tek Ka Doom *

3*1*3*1*3*	Tek Ka Doom *	Doom * Tek Ka	Doom * Doom *	Tek Ka Doom *

3*5*5*	Tek Ka Doom *	Tek Ka Tek Ka	Doom * Tek Ka	Tek Ka Doom *

1*3*1*1*1*3	Doom * Tek Ka	Doom * Doom *	Doom * Doom *	Tek Ka Doom *

5*1*5*1*	Tek Ka Tek Ka	Doom * Doom *	Tek Ka Tek Ka	Doom * Doom *

7*1*5*	Tek Ka Tek Ka	Tek Ka Doom *	Doom * Tek Ka	Tek Ka Doom *

3*5*1*3*	Tek Ka Doom *	Tek Ka Tek Ka	Doom * Doom *	Tek Ka Doom *

3*1*7*1*	Tek Ka Doom *	Doom * Tek Ka	Tek Ka Tek Ka	Doom * Doom *

3*1*1*5*1*	Tek Ka Doom *	Doom * Doom *	Tek Ka Tek Ka	Doom * Doom *

HAND DRUM NOTATION

LESSON TWO
FACTOR BY FACTOR RIGHT HAND

BASIC 3'S RIGHT HAND

3*3*3*3*	Tek Ka Doom *	Tek Ka Doom *	Tek Ka Doom *	Tek Ka Doom *
3*3*3*3*	Tek Ka Doom *	Tek Ka Doom *	Tek Ka Doom *	Tek Ka Doom *

DOUBLE 7'S RIGHT HAND

7*7*	Tek Ka Tek Ka	Tek Ka Doom *	Tek Ka Tek Ka	Tek Ka Doom *
7*7*	Tek Ka Tek Ka	Tek Ka Doom *	Tek Ka Tek Ka	Tek Ka Doom *

3-3-7 RIGHT HAND

3*3*7*	Tek Ka Doom *	Tek Ka Doom *	Tek Ka Tek Ka	Tek Ka Doom *
3*7*3*	Tek Ka Doom *	Tek Ka Tek Ka	Tek Ka Doom *	Tek Ka Doom *
7*3*3*	Tek Ka Tek Ka	Tek Ka Doom *	Tek Ka Doom *	Tek Ka Doom *

3-1-3-1-3 RIGHT HAND

3*1*3*1*3*	Tek Ka Doom *	Doom * Tek Ka	Doom * Doom *	Tek Ka Doom *
1*3*3*1*3*	Doom * Tek Ka	Doom * Tek Ka	Doom * Doom *	Tek Ka Doom *
1*3*1*3*3*	Doom * Tek Ka	Doom * Doom *	Tek Ka Doom *	Tek Ka Doom *
3*3*1*3*1*	Tek Ka Doom *	Tek Ka Doom *	Doom * Tek Ka	Doom * Doom *
3*1*3*3*1*	Tek Ka Doom *	Doom * Tek Ka	Doom * Tek Ka	Doom * Doom *
1*1*3*3*3*	Doom * Doom *	Tek Ka Doom *	Tek Ka Doom *	Tek Ka Doom *
3*1*1*3*3*	Tek Ka Doom *	Doom * Doom *	Tek Ka Doom *	Tek Ka Doom *
3*3*1*1*3*	Tek Ka Doom *	Tek Ka Doom *	Doom * Doom *	Tek Ka Doom *

HAND DRUM NOTATION

LESSON TWO
FACTOR BY FACTOR RIGHT HAND

3-5-5 RIGHT HAND

3*5*5*	Tek Ka Doom *	Tek Ka Tek Ka	Doom * Tek Ka	Tek Ka Doom *
5*3*5*	Tek Ka Tek Ka	Doom * Tek Ka	Doom * Tek Ka	Tek Ka Doom *
5*5*3*	Tek Ka Tek Ka	Doom * Tek Ka	Tek Ka Doom *	Tek Ka Doom *

1-3-1-1-1-3 RIGHT HAND

1*3*1*1*1*3	Doom * Tek Ka	Doom * Doom *	Doom * Doom *	Tek Ka Doom *
1*1*1*3*1*3	Doom * Doom *	Doom * Tek Ka	Doom * Doom *	Tek Ka Doom *
1*1*1*3*3*1	Doom * Doom *	Doom * Tek Ka	Doom * Tek Ka	Doom * Doom *
1*1*1*1*3*3	Doom * Doom *	Doom * Doom *	Tek Ka Doom *	Tek Ka Doom *
1*1*1*3*1*3	Doom * Doom *	Doom * Tek Ka	Doom * Doom *	Tek Ka Doom *
1*1*3*3*1*1	Doom * Doom *	Tek Ka Doom *	Tek Ka Doom *	Doom * Doom *
1*1*3*1*3*1	Doom * Doom *	Tek Ka Doom *	Doom * Tek Ka	Doom * Doom *
1*1*3*1*1*3	Doom * Doom *	Tek Ka Doom *	Doom * Doom *	Tek Ka Doom *
1*3*1*1*1*3	Doom * Tek Ka	Doom * Doom *	Doom * Doom *	Tek Ka Doom *
1*3*1*1*3*1	Doom * Tek Ka	Doom * Doom *	Doom * Tek Ka	Doom * Doom *
1*3*3*1*1*1	Doom * Tek Ka	Doom * Tek Ka	Doom * Doom *	Doom * Doom *
3*1*1*1*1*3	Tek Ka Doom *	Doom * Doom *	Doom * Doom *	Tek Ka Doom *
3*1*1*1*3*1	Tek Ka Doom *	Doom * Doom *	Doom * Tek Ka	Doom * Doom *
3*1*1*3*1*1	Tek Ka Doom *	Doom * Doom *	Tek Ka Doom *	Doom * Doom *
3*1*3*1*1*1	Tek Ka Doom *	Doom * Tek Ka	Doom * Doom *	Doom * Doom *

HAND DRUM NOTATION

LESSON FOUR
COMBINED FACTORS RIGHT HAND

5-1-5-1 RIGHT HAND

5*1*5*1*	Tek Ka Tek Ka	Doom * Doom *	Tek Ka Tek Ka	Doom * Doom *
5*1*1*5*	Tek Ka Tek Ka	Doom * Doom *	Doom * Tek Ka	Tek Ka Doom *
5*5*1*1*	Tek Ka Tek Ka	Doom * Tek Ka	Tek Ka Doom *	Doom * Doom *
1*1*5*5*	Doom * Doom *	Tek Ka Tek Ka	Doom * Tek Ka	Tek Ka Doom *
1*5*1*5*	Doom * Tek Ka	Tek Ka Doom *	Doom * Tek Ka	Tek Ka Doom *
1*5*5*1*	Doom * Tek Ka	Tek Ka Doom *	Tek Ka Tek Ka	Doom * Doom *

7-1-5 RIGHT HAND

7*1*5*	Tek Ka Tek Ka	Tek Ka Doom *	Doom * Tek Ka	Tek Ka Doom *
7*5*1*	Tek Ka Tek Ka	Tek Ka Doom *	Tek Ka Tek Ka	Doom * Doom *
5*7*1*	Tek Ka Tek Ka	Doom * Tek Ka	Tek Ka Tek Ka	Doom * Doom *
5*1*7*	Tek Ka Tek Ka	Doom * Doom *	Tek Ka Tek Ka	Tek Ka Doom *
1*7*5*	Doom * Tek Ka	Tek Ka Tek Ka	Doom * Tek Ka	Tek Ka Doom *
1*5*7*	Doom * Tek Ka	Tek Ka Doom *	Tek Ka Tek Ka	Tek Ka Doom *

HAND DRUM NOTATION

LESSON FOUR
COMBINED FACTORS RIGHT HAND

3-5-1-3 RIGHT HAND

3*5*1*3*	Tek Ka Doom *	Tek Ka Tek Ka	Doom * Doom *	Tek Ka Doom *
5*1*3*3*	Tek Ka Tek Ka	Doom * Doom *	Tek Ka Doom *	Tek Ka Doom *
1*3*3*5*	Doom * Tek Ka	Doom * Tek Ka	Doom * Tek Ka	Tek Ka Doom *
1*3*5*3*	Doom * Tek Ka	Doom * Tek Ka	Tek Ka Doom *	Tek Ka Doom *
1*5*3*3*	Doom * Tek Ka	Tek Ka Doom *	Tek Ka Doom *	Tek Ka Doom *
5*3*3*1*	Tek Ka Tek Ka	Doom * Tek Ka	Doom * Tek Ka	Doom * Doom *
5*3*1*3*	Tek Ka Tek Ka	Doom * Tek Ka	Doom * Doom *	Tek Ka Doom *
3*1*5*3*	Tek Ka Doom *	Doom * Tek Ka	Tek Ka Doom *	Tek Ka Doom *
3*3*1*5*	Tek Ka Doom *	Tek Ka Doom *	Doom * Tek Ka	Tek Ka Doom *
3*5*3*1*	Tek Ka Doom *	Tek Ka Tek Ka	Doom * Tek Ka	Doom * Doom *

3-1-7-1 RIGHT HAND

3*1*7*1*	Tek Ka Doom *	Doom * Tek Ka	Tek Ka Tek Ka	Doom * Doom *
3*1*1*7*	Tek Ka Doom *	Doom * Doom *	Tek Ka Tek Ka	Tek Ka Doom *
3*7*1*1*	Tek Ka Doom *	Tek Ka Tek Ka	Tek Ka Doom *	Doom * Doom *
7*1*1*3*	Tek Ka Tek Ka	Tek Ka Doom *	Doom * Doom *	Tek Ka Doom *
7*1*3*1*	Tek Ka Tek Ka	Tek Ka Doom *	Doom * Tek Ka	Doom * Doom *
7*3*1*1*	Tek Ka Tek Ka	Tek Ka Doom *	Tek Ka Doom *	Doom * Doom *
1*3*7*1*	Doom * Tek Ka	Doom * Tek Ka	Tek Ka Tek Ka	Tek Ka Doom *
1*3*1*7*	Doom * Tek Ka	Doom * Doom *	Tek Ka Tek Ka	Tek Ka Doom *
1*7*1*3*	Doom * Tek Ka	Tek Ka Tek Ka	Doom * Doom *	Tek Ka Doom *

HAND DRUM NOTATION

LESSON FOUR
COMBINED FACTORS RIGHT HAND

3-1-1-5-1 RIGHT HAND

3*1*1*5*1*	Tek Ka Doom *	Doom * Doom *	Tek Ka Tek Ka	Doom * Doom *
3*1*1*1*5*	Tek Ka Doom *	Doom * Doom *	Doom * Tek Ka	Tek Ka Doom *
3*1*5*1*1*	Tek Ka Doom *	Doom * Tek Ka	Tek Ka Doom *	Doom * Doom *
3*5*1*1*1*	Tek Ka Doom *	Tek Ka Tek Ka	Doom * Doom *	Doom * Doom *
5*3*1*1*1*	Tek Ka Tek Ka	Doom * Tek Ka	Doom * Doom *	Doom * Doom *
5*1*1*1*3*	Tek Ka Tek Ka	Doom * Doom *	Doom * Doom *	Tek Ka Doom *
5*1*1*3*1*	Tek Ka Tek Ka	Doom * Doom *	Doom * Tek Ka	Doom * Doom *
5*1*3*1*1*	Tek Ka Tek Ka	Doom * Doom *	Tek Ka Doom *	Doom * Doom *
1*5*1*1*3*	Doom * Tek Ka	Tek Ka Doom *	Doom * Doom *	Tek Ka Doom *
1*5*1*3*1*	Doom * Tek Ka	Tek Ka Doom *	Doom * Tek Ka	Doom * Doom *
1*5*3*1*1*	Doom * Tek Ka	Tek Ka Doom *	Tek Ka Doom *	Doom * Doom *
1*3*5*1*1*	Doom * Tek Ka	Doom * Tek Ka	Tek Ka Doom *	Doom * Doom *
1*3*1*1*5*	Doom * Tek Ka	Doom * Doom *	Doom * Tek Ka	Tek Ka Doom *
1*3*1*5*1*	Doom * Tek Ka	Doom * Doom *	Tek Ka Tek Ka	Doom * Doom *
1*1*5*3*1*	Doom * Doom *	Tek Ka Tek Ka	Doom * Tek Ka	Doom * Doom *
1*1*5*1*3*	Doom * Doom *	Tek Ka Tek Ka	Doom * Doom *	Tek Ka Doom *
1*1*3*5*1*	Doom * Doom *	Tek Ka Doom *	Tek Ka Tek Ka	Doom * Doom *
1*1*3*1*5*	Doom * Doom *	Tek Ka Doom *	Doom * Tek Ka	Tek Ka Doom *
1*1*1*3*5*	Doom * Doom *	Doom * Tek Ka	Doom * Tek Ka	Tek Ka Doom *

SECTION 4

SYNCOPATION

SYNCOPATION

INTRODUCTION TO SYNCOPATED RHYTHMS

In syncopated factors, the accent is an un-played note marked as an elevated pause ^
Two syncopated rhythms in this course are- SYNCOPATED 4 and SYNCOPATED 2

SYNCOPATED 4
SYNC 4 NOTATION   RL^LR * RL^LR * RL^LR * RL^LR *

The accent is on the un-played note between four played notes in the sequence RL^LR*
SYNC 4 contains six sixteenth notes.
The first two notes are played RL
The middle note carrying the accent is assigned the symbol   ^
Then the final notes are played LR.
SYNCOPATED 4 is always followed by a silent note, a rest marked *

SPEAKING SYNCOPATED 4- Speak the phrase- "right, left ^ left right"
        Starting with a low pitch "right" then lift your pitch "left"
        Hold the center pause like an elevated suspense
        Then start high again "left" and drop pitch down again "right"

SYNCOPATED 2
SYNC 2 NOTATION   RR^ * RR^ * RR^ * RR^ *

The accent is on an un-played note just after the two played notes in the sequence RR^*
This rhythm occupies four sixteenth notes and may be played on its own as straight 2's
or paired with other factors to form patterns.
The two played notes are played one after the other.
The final silent note is still part of the numeric piece.
SYNCOPATED 2 is always followed by a silent note marked *

SPEAKING SYNCOPATED 2- Speak the phrase- "right, right ^ * "right, right ^ *
        Starting with a swift abrupt "right" "right" with a stomping feeling
        Hold the pause note in elevated suspense
        Then hold the rest note resolving the suspense

SYNCOPATION

SYNCOPATED RHYTHMS LESSON BY LESSON

SYNCOPATED 4'S

LESSON ONE- Syncopated 4 Basics Right and Left

LESSON TWO- Syncopated 4 Tables Right

LESSON THREE- Syncopated 4 Tables Left

SYNCOPATED 2'S

LESSON FOUR- Syncopated 2 Basics Right and Left

LESSON FIVE- Syncopated 2 Tables Right

LESSON SIX- Syncopated 2 Tables Left

SYNCOPATED 2'S AND 4'S

LESSON SEVEN- Syncopated 2&4 Basics Right and Left

LESSON EIGHT- Syncopated 2 & 4 Tables Right

LESSON NINE- Syncopated 2 & 4 Tables Left

SYNCOPATION
SYNCOPATED 4 BASICS INTRODUCTION

SYNCOPATED 4
SYNCOPATED 4- the accent is on an un-played note
Falling between the four played notes in the sequence RL^LR

    The first two notes are played RL
    The middle note carrying the accent is assigned the symbol ^
    Then the final notes are played LR.

SYNCOPATED 4 is always followed by a silent note marked *

SYNCOPATED 4 looks like RL^LR * RL^LR * RL^LR * RL^LR *

Rule of odds and evens
SYNCOPATED 4 represents six sixteenth notes
Counting SYNC 4

1	Right
2	Left
3	^ Pause
4	Left
5	Right
6	* Rest

Speak the phrase "right, left ^ left right *
    Starting with a low pitch "right" and lift your pitch "left"
    Hold the center pause like and elevated suspense
    Then start high again "left and drop pitch down again "right"

These rhythms are difficult to hear and to count.
Remember the following phrase

"AND A ONE-E, AND A TWO-E, AND A THREE-E, AND A FOUR- E"

SYNCOPATION

LESSON ONE

SYNCOPATED 4 BASICS RIGHT AND LEFT

SYNCOPATED 4 BASICS
RIGHT HAND

3*4*4*	R L R *	R L ^ L	R * R L	^ L R *

3*4*1*3*	R L R *	R L ^ L	R * R *	R L R *

5*1*4*1*	R L R L	R * R *	R L ^ L	R * R *

3*4*5*	R L R *	R L ^ L	R * R L	R L R *

1*4*7*	R * R L	^ L R *	R L R L	R L R *

4*4*1*1*	R L ^ L	R * R L	^ L R *	R * R *

3*1*4*1*1*	R L R *	R * R L	^ L R *	R * R *

SYNCOPATION

LESSON ONE
SYNCOPATED 4 BASICS RIGHT AND LEFT

SYNCOPATED 4 BASICS
LEFT HAND

3*4*4*	L R L *	L R ^ R	L * L R	^ R L *
3*4*1*3*	L R L *	L R ^ R	L * L *	L R L *
5*1*4*1*	L R L R	L * L *	L R ^ R	L * L *
3*4*5*	L R L *	L R ^ R	L * L R	L R L *
1*4*7*	L * L R	^ R L *	L R L R	L R L *
4*4*1*1*	L R ^ R	L * L R	^ R L *	L * L *
3*1*4*1*1*	L R L *	L * L R	^ R L *	L * L *

SYNCOPATION

LESSON TWO

SYNCOPATED 4 TABLES RIGHT

3-4-4 RIGHT HAND

3*4*4*	R L R *	R L ^ L	R * R L	^ L R *
4*4*3*	R L ^ L	R * R L	^ L R *	R L R *
4*3*4*	R L ^ L	R * R L	R * R L	^ L R *

3-4-1-3 RIGHT HAND

3*4*1*3*	R L R *	R L ^ L	R * R *	R L R *
3*4*3*1*	R L R*	R L ^ L	R * R L	R * R *
3*1*3*4*	R L R *	R * R L	R * R L	^ L R *
4*3*3*1*	R L ^ L	R * R L	R * R L	R * R *
3*1*4*3*	R L R *	R * R L	^ L R *	R L R *
4*3*1*3*	R L ^ L	R * R L	R * R *	R L R *
1*3*3*4*	R * R L	R * R L	R * R L	^ L R *
4*1*3*3*	R L ^ L	R * R *	R L R *	R L R *
1*3*4*3*	R * R L	R * R L	^ L R *	R L R *
1*4*3*3*	R * R L	^ L R *	R L R *	R L R *

RHYTHM FACTORING

SYNCOPATION

LESSON TWO

SYNCOPATED 4 TABLES RIGHT

5-1-4-1 RIGHT HAND

5*1*4*1*	R L R L	R * R *	R L ^ L	R * R *
5*4*1*1*	R L R L	R * R L	^ L R *	R * R *
5*1*1*4*	R L R L	R * R *	R * R L	^ L R *
4*1*1*5*	R L ^ L	R * R *	R * R L	R L R *
4*1*5*1*	R L ^ L	R * R *	R L R L	R * R *
4*5*1*1*	R L ^ L	R * R L	R L R *	R * R *
1*4*5*1*	R * R L	^ L R *	R L R L	R * R *
1*4*1*5*	R * R L	^ L R *	R * R L	R L R *
1*5*4*1*	R * R L	R L R *	R L ^ L	R * R *
1*5*1*4*	R * R L	R L R *	R * R L	^ L R *
1*1*5*4*	R * R *	R L R L	R * R L	^ L R *
1*1*4*5*	R * R *	R L ^ L	R * R L	R L R *

3-4-5 RIGHT HAND

3*4*5*	R L R *	R L ^ L	R * R L	R L R *
3*5*4*	R L R *	R L R L	R * R L	^ L R *
4*3*5*	R L ^ L	R * R L	R * R L	R L R *
4*5*3*	R L ^ L	R * R L	R L R *	R L R *
5*3*4*	R L R L	R * R L	R * R L	^ L R *
5*4*3*	R L R L	R * R L	^ L R *	R L R *

RHYTHM FACTORING

SYNCOPATION

LESSON TWO

SYNCOPATED 4 TABLES RIGHT

1-4-7 RIGHT HAND

1*4*7*	R * R L	^ L R *	R L R L	R L R *
1*7*4*	R * R L	R L R L	R * R L	^ L R *
4*1*7*	R L ^ L	R * R *	R L R L	R L R *
4*7*1*	R L ^ L	R * R L	R L R L	R * R *
7*1*4*	R L R L	R L R *	R * R L	^ L R *
7*4*1*	R L R L	R L R *	R L ^ L	R * R *

4-4-1-1 RIGHT HAND

4*4*1*1*	R L ^ L	R * R L	^ L R *	R * R *
4*1*4*1*	R L ^ L	R * R *	R L ^ L	R * R *
4*1*1*4*	R L ^ L	R * R *	R * R L	^ L R *
1*4*4*1*	R * R L	^ L R *	R L ^ L	R * R *
1*4*1*4*	R * R L	^ L R *	R * R L	^ L R *
1*1*4*4*	R * R *	R L ^ L	R * R L	^ L R *

SYNCOPATION

LESSON TWO
SYNCOPATED 4 TABLES RIGHT

3-1-4-1-1   RIGHT HAND

3*1*4*1*1*	R L R *	R * R L	^ L R *	R * R *
3*4*1*1*1*	R L R *	R L ^ L	R * R *	R * R *
3*1*1*4*1*	R L R *	R * R *	R L ^ L	R * R *
3*1*1*1*4	R L R *	R * R *	R * R L	^ L R *
4*3*1*1*1*	R L ^ L	R * R L	R * R *	R * R *
4*1*3*1*1*	R L ^ L	R * R *	R L R *	R * R *
4*1*1*3*1*	R L ^ L	R * R *	R * R L	R * R *
4*1*1*1*3*	R L ^ L	R * R *	R * R *	R L R *
1*1*1*4*3*	R * R *	R * R L	^ L R *	R L R *
1*1*1*3*4	R * R *	R * R L	R * R L	^ L R *
1*1*4*1*3*	R * R *	R L ^ L	R * R *	R L R *
1*4*1*1*3*	R * R L	^ L R *	R * R *	R L R *
1*4*1*3*1*	R * R L	^ L R *	R * R L	R * R *
1*4*3*1*1*	R * R L	^ L R *	R L R *	R * R *
1*1*4*3*1*	R * R *	R L ^ L	R * R L	R * R *
1*1*3*4*1*	R * R *	R L R *	R L ^ L	R * R *
1*1*3*1*4	R * R *	R L R *	R * R L	^ L R *
1*3*4*1*1*	R * R L	R * R L	^ L R *	R * R *
1*3*1*4*1*	R * R L	R * R *	R L ^ L	R * R *
1*3*1*1*4*	R * R L	R * R *	R * R L	^ L R *

SYNCOPATION

LESSON THREE
SYNCOPATED 4 TABLES LEFT

3-4-4 LEFT HAND

3*4*4*	L R L *	L R ^ R	L * L R	^ R L *
4*4*3*	L R ^ R	L * L R	^ R L *	L R L *
4*3*4*	L R ^ R	L * L R	L * L R	^ R L *

3-4-1-3 LEFT HAND

3*4*1*3*	L R L *	L R ^ R	L * L *	L R L *
3*4*3*1*	L R L *	L R ^ R	L * L R	L * L *
3*1*3*4*	L R L *	L * L R	L * L R	^ R L *
4*3*3*1*	L R ^ R	L * L R	L * L R	L * L *
3*1*4*3*	L R L *	L * L R	^ R L *	L R L *
4*3*1*3*	L R ^ R	L * L R	L * L *	L R L *
1*3*3*4*	L * L R	L * L R	L * L R	^ R L *
4*1*3*3*	L R ^ R	L * L *	L R L *	L R L *
1*3*4*3*	L * L R	L * L R	^ R L *	L R L *
1*4*3*3*	L * L R	^ R L *	L R L *	L R L *

SYNCOPATION

LESSON THREE
SYNCOPATED 4 TABLES RIGHT

5-1-4-1 LEFT HAND

5*1*4*1*	L R L R	L * L *	L R ^ R	L * L *
5*4*1*1*	L R L R	L * L R	^ R L *	L * L *
5*1*1*4*	L R L R	L * L *	L * L R	^ R L *
4*1*1*5*	L R ^ R	L * L *	L * L R	L R L *
4*1*5*1*	L R ^ R	L * L *	L R L R	L * L *
4*5*1*1*	L R ^ R	L * L R	L R L *	L * L *
1*4*5*1*	L * L R	^ R L *	L R L R	L * L *
1*4*1*5*	L * L R	^ R L *	L * L R	L R L *
1*5*4*1*	L * L R	L R L *	L R ^ R	L * L *
1*5*1*4*	L * L R	L R L *	L * L R	^ R L *
1*1*5*4*	L * L *	L R L R	L * L R	^ R L *
1*1*4*5*	L * L *	L R ^ R	L *L R	L R L *

3-4-5 LEFT HAND

3*4*5*	L R L *	L R ^ R	L * L R	L R L *
3*5*4*	L R L *	L R L R	L * L R	^ R L *
4*3*5*	L R ^ R	L * L R	L * L R	L R L *
4*5*3*	L R ^ R	L * L R	L R L *	L R L *
5*3*4*	L R L R	L * L R	L * L R	^ R L *
5*4*3*	L R L R	L * L R	^ R L *	L R L *

SYNCOPATION

LESSON THREE
SYNCOPATED 4 TABLES RIGHT

1-4-7 LEFT HAND

1*4*7*	L * L R	^ R L *	L R L R	L R L *
1*7*4*	L * L R	L R L R	L * L R	^ R L *
4*1*7*	L R ^ R	L * L *	L R L R	L R L *
4*7*1*	L R ^ R	L * L R	L R L R	L * L *
7*1*4*	L R L R	L R L *	L * L R	^ R L *
7*4*1*	L R L R	L R L *	L R ^ R	L * L *

4-4-1-1 LEFT HAND

4*4*1*1*	L R ^ R	L * L R	^ R L *	L * L *
4*1*4*1*	L R ^ R	L * L *	L R ^ R	L * L *
4*1*1*4*	L R ^ R	L * L *	L * L R	^ R L *
1*4*4*1*	L * L R	^ R L *	L R ^ R	L * L *
1*4*1*4*	L * L R	^ R L *	L * L R	^ R L *
1*1*4*4*	L * L *	L R ^ R	L * L R	^ R L *

SYNCOPATION

LESSON THREE
SYNCOPATED 4 TABLES RIGHT

3-1-4-1-1 LEFT HAND

3*1*4*1*1*	L R L *	L * L R	^ R L *	L * L *
3*4*1*1*1*	L R L *	L R ^ R	L * L *	L * L *
3*1*1*4*1*	L R L *	L * L *	L R ^ R	L * L *
3*1*1*1*4	L R L *	L * L *	L * L R	^ R L *
4*3*1*1*1*	L R ^ R	L * L R	L * L *	L * L *
4*1*3*1*1*	L R ^ R	L * L *	L R L *	L * L *
4*1*1*3*1*	L R ^ R	L * L *	L * L R	L * L *
4*1*1*1*3	L R ^ R	L * L *	L * L *	L R L *
1*1*1*4*3*	L * L *	L * L R	^ R L *	L R L *
1*1*1*3*4	L * L *	L * L R	L * L R	^ R L *
1*1*4*1*3*	L * L *	L R ^ R	L * L *	L R L *
1*4*1*1*3	L * L R	^ R L *	L * L *	L R L *
1*4*1*3*1*	L * L R	^ R L *	L * L R	L * L *
1*4*3*1*1*	L * L R	^ R L *	L R L *	L * L *
1*1*4*3*1*	L * L *	L R ^ R	L * L R	L * L *
1*1*3*4*1*	L * L *	L R L *	L R ^ R	L * L *
1*1*3*1*4	L * L *	L R L *	L * L R	^ R L *
1*3*4*1*1*	L * L R	L * L R	^ R L *	L * L *
1*3*1*4*1*	L * L R	L * L *	L R ^ R	L * L *
1*3*1*1*4	L * L R	L * L *	L * L R	^ R L *

SYNCOPATION
SYNCOPATED 2 BASICS INTRODUCTION

SYNCOPATED 2
SYNCOPATED 2 rhythms have a rushed, stomping feeling.
The accent is on an un-played note just after the two played notes.

The two notes are played one after the other.
The silent pause note is the third beat of the numeric piece.

SYNCOPATED 2 is always followed by a silent rest ncte marked *

SYNCOPATED 2 looks like this: RR^ * RR^ * RR^ * RR^ *

Rule of odds and evens
SYNCOPATED 2 represents 4 Sixteenth notes
Counting SYNC 2

1	Right
2	Right
3	^ Pause
4	* Rest

Speak the phrase "right, right ^ *
     Starting with a swift abrupt "right" "right" with a stomping feeling
     Hold the pause like and elevated suspense
     Then hold the rest note releasing Tension

These rhythms are difficult to hear and to count.
Remember the following phrase

"AND A ONE-E, AND A TWO-E, AND A THREE-E, AND A FOUR- E"

RHYTHM FACTORING

SYNCOPATION

LESSON FOUR
SYNCOPATED 2 BASICS RIGHT AND LEFT

SYNCOPATED 2 BASICS
RIGHT HAND

2*2*2*2*	R R ^ *	R R ^ *	R R ^ *	R R ^ *
2*2*7*	R R ^ *	R R ^ *	R L R L	R L R *
2*3*7*	R R ^ *	R L R *	R L R L	R L R *
2*5*5	R R ^ *	R L R L	R * R L	R L R *
3*2*2*3*	R L R *	R R ^ *	R R ^ *	R L R *
3*1*2*1*2*	R L R *	R * R R	^ * R *	R R ^ *
2*1*2*1*2*	R R ^ *	R * R R	^ * R *	R R ^ *
3*2*2*2*	R L R *	R R ^ *	R R ^ *	R R ^ *
5*1*2*3*	R L R L	R * R *	R R ^ *	R L R *
3*2*3*1*1*	R L R *	R R ^ *	R L R *	R * R *
2*7*1*1*	R R ^ *	R L R L	R L R *	R * R *
5*1*2*2*	R L R L	R * R *	R R ^ *	R R ^ *

SYNCOPATION

LESSON FOUR
SYNCOPATED 2 BASICS RIGHT AND LEFT

SYNCOPATED 2 BASICS
LEFT HAND

2*2*2*2*	L L ^ *	L L ^ *	L L ^ *	L L ^ *
2*2*7*	L L ^ *	L L ^ *	L R L R	L R L *
2*3*7*	L L ^ *	L R L *	L R L R	L R L *
2*5*5	L L ^ *	L R L R	L * L R	L R L *
3*2*2*3*	L R L *	L L ^ *	L L ^ *	L R L *
3*1*2*1*2*	L R L *	L * L L	^ * L *	L L ^ *
2*1*2*1*2*	L L ^ *	L * L L	^ * L *	L L ^ *
3*2*2*2*	L R L *	L L ^ *	L L ^ *	L L ^ *
5*1*2*3*	L R L R	L * L *	L L ^ *	L R L *
3*2*3*1*1*	L R L *	L L ^ *	L R L *	L * L *
2*7*1*1*	L L ^ *	L R L R	L R L *	L * L *
5*1*2*2*	L R L R	L * L *	L L ^ *	L L ^ *

RHYTHM FACTORING

SYNCOPATION

LESSON FIVE
SYNCOPATED 2 BASICS RIGHT

2-2-7 RIGHT HAND

2*2*7*	R R ^ *	R R ^ *	R L R L	R L R *
2*7*2*	R R ^ *	R L R L	R L R *	R R ^ *
7*2*2*	R L R L	R L R *	R R ^ *	R R ^ *

2-3-7 RIGHT HAND

2*3*7*	R R ^ *	R L R *	R L R L	R L R *
2*7*3*	R R ^ *	R L R L	R L R *	R L R *
3*2*7*	R L R *	R R ^ *	R L R L	R L R *
3*7*2*	R L R *	R L R L	R L R *	R R ^ *
7*3*2*	R L R L	R L R *	R L R *	R R ^ *
7*2*3*	R L R L	R L R *	R R ^ *	R L R *

2-5-5 RIGHT HAND

2*5*5*	R R ^ *	R L R L	R * R L	R L R *
5*5*2*	R L R L	R * R L	R L R *	R R ^ *
5*2*5*	R L R L	R * R R	^ * R L	R L R *

SYNCOPATION

LESSON FIVE
SYNCOPATED 2 BASICS RIGHT

3-2-2-3 RIGHT HAND

3*2*2*3*	R L R *	R R ^ *	R R ^ *	R L R *
3*2*3*2*	R L R *	R R ^ *	R L R *	R R ^ *
3*3*2*2*	R L R *	R L R *	R R ^ *	R R ^ *
2*2*3*3*	R R ^ *	R R ^ *	R L R *	R L R *
2*3*2*3*	R R ^ *	R L R *	R R ^ *	R L R *
2*3*3*2*	R R ^ *	R L R *	R L R *	R R ^ *

3-1-2-1-2 RIGHT HAND

3*1*2*1*2*	R L R *	R * R R	^ * R *	R R ^ *
3*1*2*2*1*	R L R *	R * R R	^ * R R	^ * R *
3*1*1*2*2*	R L R *	R * R *	R R ^ *	R R ^ *
3*2*2*1*1*	R L R *	R R ^ *	R R ^ *	R * R *
3*2*1*2*1*	R L R *	R R ^ *	R * R R	^ * R *
3*2*1*1*2*	R L R *	R R ^ *	R * R *	R R ^ *
2*3*1*1*2*	R R ^ *	R L R *	R * R *	R R ^ *
2*3*1*2*1*	R R ^ *	R L R *	R * R R	^ * R *
2*3*2*1*1*	R R ^ *	R L R *	R R ^ *	R * R *
2*1*2*3*1*	R R ^ *	R * R R	^ * R L	R * R *
1*2*3*1*2*	R * R R	^ * R L	R * R *	R R ^ *
1*3*1*2*2*	R * R L	R * R *	R R ^ *	R R ^ *

SYNCOPATION

LESSON FIVE
SYNCOPATED 2 BASICS RIGHT

2-1-2-1-2 RIGHT HAND

2*1*2*1*2*	R R ^ *	R * R R	^ * R *	R R ^ *
2*1*2*2*1*	R R ^ *	R * R R	^ * R R	^ * R *
2*1*1*2*2*	R R ^ *	R * R *	R R ^ *	R R ^ *
2*2*2*1*1*	R R ^ *	R R ^ *	R R ^ *	R * R *
2*2*1*2*1*	R R ^ *	R R ^ *	R * R R	^ * R *
2*2*1*1*2*	R R ^ *	R R ^ *	R * R *	R R ^ *
1*1*2*2*2*	R * R *	R R ^ *	R R ^ *	R R ^ *
1*2*1*2*2*	R * R R	^ * R *	R R ^ *	R R ^ *
1*2*2*1*2*	R * R R	^ * R R	^ * R *	R R ^ *

3-2-2-2 RIGHT HAND

3*2*2*2*	R L R *	R R ^ *	R R ^ *	R R ^ *
2*3*2*2*	R R ^ *	R L R *	R R ^ *	R R ^ *
2*2*3*2*	R R ^ *	R R ^ *	R L R *	R R ^ *
2*2*2*3*	R R ^ *	R R ^ *	R R ^ *	R L R *

SYNCOPATION

LESSON FIVE
SYNCOPATED 2 BASICS RIGHT

5-1-2-3 RIGHT HAND

5*1*2*3*	R L R L	R * R *	R R ^ *	R L R *
5*1*3*2*	R L R L	R * R *	R L R *	R R ^ *
5*2*3*1*	R L R L	R * R R	^ * R L	R * R *
5*2*1*3*	R L R L	R * R R	^ * R *	R L R *
5*3*2*1*	R L R L	R * R L	R * R R	^ * R *
5*3*1*2*	R L R L	R * R L	R * R *	R R ^ *
2*1*3*5*	R R ^ *	R * R L	R * R L	R L R *
2*1*5*3*	R R ^ *	R * R L	R L R *	R L R *
2*3*5*1*	R R ^ *	R L R *	R L R L	R * R *
2*3*1*5*	R R ^ *	R L R *	R * R L	R L R *
2*5*1*3*	R R ^ *	R L R L	R * R *	R L R *
2*5*3*1*	R R ^ *	R L R L	R * R L	R * R *
1*2*3*5*	R * R R	^ * R L	R * R L	R L R *
1*2*5*3*	R * R R	^ * R L	R L R *	R L R *
1*3*5*2*	R * R L	R * R L	R L R *	R R ^ *
1*3*2*5*	R * R L	R * R R	^ * R L	R L R *
1*5*3*2*	R * R L	R L R *	R L R *	R R ^ *
1*5*2*3*	R * R L	R L R *	R R ^ *	R L R *
3*5*2*1*	R L R *	R L R L	R * R R	^ * R *
3*5*1*2*	R L R *	R L R L	R * R *	R R ^ *
3*1*2*5*	R L R *	R * R R	^ * R L	R L R *

SYNCOPATION

LESSON FIVE
SYNCOPATED 2 BASICS RIGHT

3-2-3-1-1 RIGHT HAND

3*2*3*1*1*	R L R *	R R ^ *	R L R *	R * R *
3*2*1*3*1*	R L R *	R R ^ *	R * R L	R * R *
3*2*1*1*3*	R L R *	R R ^ *	R * R *	R L R *
3*3*1*1*2*	R L R *	R L R *	R * R *	R R ^ *
3*3*1*2*1*	R L R *	R L R *	R * R R	^ * R *
3*3*2*1*1*	R L R *	R L R *	R R ^ *	R * R *
2*3*3*1*1*	R R ^ *	R L R *	R L R *	R * R *
2*3*1*3*1*	R R ^ *	R L R *	R * R L	R * R *
2*3*1*1*3*	R R ^ *	R L R *	R * R *	R L R *
2*1*1*3*3*	R R ^ *	R * R *	R L R *	R L R *
2*1*3*1*3*	R R ^ *	R * R L	R * R *	R L R *
2*1*3*3*1*	R R ^ *	R * R L	R * R L	R * R *
1*2*3*3*1*	R * R R	^ * R L	R * R L	R * R *
1*2*3*1*3*	R * R R	^ * R L	R * R *	R L R *
1*2*1*3*3*	R * R R	^ * R *	R L R *	R L R *
1*1*3*3*2*	R * R *	R L R *	R L R *	R R ^ *
1*1*3*2*3*	R * R *	R L R *	R R ^ *	R L R *
1*1*2*3*3*	R * R *	R R ^ *	R L R *	R L R *
1*3*2*3*1*	R * R L	R * R R	^ * R L	R * R *
1*3*2*1*3*	R * R L	R * R R	^ * R *	R L R *
1*3*1*2*3*	R * R L	R * R *	R R ^ *	R L R *

RHYTHM FACTORING

SYNCOPATION

LESSON FIVE
SYNCOPATED 2 BASICS RIGHT

2-7-1-1 RIGHT HAND

2*7*1*1*	R R ^ *	R L R L	R L R *	R * R *
2*1*7*1*	R R ^ *	R * R L	R L R L	R * R *
2*1*1*7*	R R ^ *	R * R *	R L R L	R L R *
7*1*1*2*	R L R L	R L R *	R * R *	R R ^ *
7*1*2*1*	R L R L	R L R *	R * R R	^ * R *
7*2*1*1*	R L R L	R L R *	R R ^ *	R * R *
2*7*1*1*	R R ^ *	R L R L	R L L *	R * R *
2*1*7*1*	R R ^ *	R * R L	R L R L	R * R *
2*1*1*7*	R R ^ *	R * R *	R L R L	R L R *

5-1-2-2 RIGHT HAND

5*1*2*2*	R L R L	R * R *	R R ^ *	R R ^ *
5*2*1*2*	R L R L	R * R R	^ * R *	R R ^ *
5*2*2*1*	R L R L	R * R R	^ * R R	^ * R *
2*1*5*2*	R R ^ *	R * R L	R L R *	R R ^ *
2*1*2*5*	R R ^ *	R * R R	^ * R L	R L R *
2*5*2*1*	R R ^ *	R L R L	R * R R	^ * R *
2*5*1*2*	R R ^ *	R L R L	R * R *	R R ^ *
1*5*2*2*	R * R L	R L R *	R R ^ *	R R ^ *
1*2*5*2*	R * R R	^ * R L	R L R *	R R ^ *
1*2*2*5*	R * R R	^ * R R	^ * R L	R L R *

SYNCOPATION

LESSON SIX
SYNCOPATED 2 BASICS LEFT

2-2-7 LEFT HAND

2*2*7*	L L ^ *	L L ^ *	L R L R	L R L *
2*7*2*	L L ^ *	L R L R	L R L *	L L ^ *
7*2*2*	L R L R	L R L *	L L ^ *	L L ^ *

2-3-7 LEFT HAND

2*3*7*	L L ^ *	L R L *	L R L R	L R L *
2*7*3*	L L ^ *	L R L R	L R L *	L R L *
3*2*7*	L R L *	L L ^ *	L R L R	L R L *
3*7*2*	L R L *	L R L R	L R L *	L L ^ *
7*3*2*	L R L R	L R L *	L R L *	L L ^ *
7*2*3*	L R L R	L R L *	L L ^ *	L R L *

2-5-5 LEFT HAND

2*5*5*	L L ^ *	L R L R	L * L R	L R L *
5*5*2*	L R L R	L * L R	L R L *	L L ^ *
5*2*5*	L R L R	L * L L	^ * L R	L R L *

SYNCOPATION

LESSON SIX
SYNCOPATED 2 BASICS LEFT

3-2-2-3 LEFT HAND

3*2*2*3*	L R L *	L L ^ *	L L ^ *	L R L *
3*2*3*2*	L R L *	L L ^ *	L R L *	L L ^ *
3*3*2*2*	L R L *	L R L *	L L ^ *	L L ^ *
2*2*3*3*	L L ^ *	L L ^ *	L R L *	L R L *
2*3*2*3*	L L ^ *	L R L *	L L ^ *	L R L *
2*3*3*2*	L L ^ *	L R L *	L R L *	L L ^ *

3-1-2-1-2 LEFT HAND

3*1*2*1*2*	L R L *	L * L L	^ * L *	L L ^ *
3*1*2*2*1*	L R L *	L * L L	^ * L L	^ * L *
3*1*1*2*2*	L R L *	L * L *	L L ^ *	L L ^ *
3*2*2*1*1*	L R L *	L L ^ *	L L ^ *	L * L *
3*2*1*2*1*	L R L *	L L ^ *	L * L L	^ * L *
3*2*1*1*2*	L R L *	L L ^ *	L * L *	L L ^ *
2*3*1*1*2*	L L ^ *	L R L *	L * L *	L L ^ *
2*3*1*2*1*	L L ^ *	L R L *	L * L L	^ * L *
2*3*2*1*1*	L L ^ *	L R L *	L L ^ *	L * L *
2*1*2*3*1*	L L ^ *	L * L L	^ * L R	L * L *
1*2*3*1*2*	L * L L	^ * L R	L * L *	L L ^ *
1*3*1*2*2*	L * L R	L * L *	L L ^ *	L L ^ *

SYNCOPATION

LESSON SIX
SYNCOPATED 2 BASICS LEFT

2-1-2-1-2 LEFT HAND

2*1*2*1*2*	L L ^ *	L * L L	^ * L *	L L ^ *
2*1*2*2*1*	L L ^ *	L * L L	^ * L L	^ * L *
2*1*1*2*2*	L L ^ *	L * L *	L L ^ *	L L ^ *
2*2*2*1*1*	L L ^ *	L L ^ *	L L ^ *	L * L *
2*2*1*2*1*	L L ^ *	L L ^ *	L * L L	^ * L *
2*2*1*1*2*	L L ^ *	L L ^ *	L * L *	L L ^ *
1*1*2*2*2*	L * L *	L L ^ *	L L ^ *	L L ^ *
1*2*1*2*2*	L * L L	^ * L *	L L ^ *	L L ^ *
1*2*2*1*2*	L * L L	^ * L L	^ * L *	L L ^ *

3-2-2-2 LEFT HAND

3*2*2*2*	L R L *	L L ^ *	L L ^ *	L L ^ *
2*3*2*2*	L L ^ *	L R L *	L L ^ *	L L ^ *
2*2*3*2*	L L ^ *	L L ^ *	L R L *	L L ^ *
2*2*2*3*	L L ^ *	L L ^ *	L L ^ *	L R L *

SYNCOPATION

LESSON SIX
SYNCOPATED 2 BASICS LEFT

5-1-2-3 LEFT HAND

5*1*2*3*	L R L R	L * L *	L L ^ *	L R L *
5*1*3*2*	L R L R	L * L *	L R L *	L L ^ *
5*2*3*1*	L R L R	L * L L	^ * L R	L * L *
5*2*1*3*	L R L R	L * L L	^ * L *	L R L *
5*3*2*1*	L R L R	L * L R	L * L L	^ * L *
5*3*1*2*	L R L R	L * L R	L * L *	L L ^ *
2*1*3*5*	L L ^ *	L * L R	L * L R	L R L *
2*1*5*3*	L L ^ *	L * L R	L R L *	L R L *
2*3*5*1*	L L ^ *	L R L *	L R L R	L * L *
2*3*1*5*	L L ^ *	L R L *	L * L R	L R L *
2*5*1*3*	L L ^ *	L R L R	L * L *	L R L *
2*5*3*1*	L L ^ *	L R L R	L * L R	L * L *
1*2*3*5*	L * L L	^ * L R	L * L R	L R L *
1*2*5*3*	L * L L	^ * L R	L R L *	L R L *
1*3*5*2*	L * L R	L * L R	L R L *	L L ^ *
1*3*2*5*	L * L R	L * L L	^ * L R	L R L *
1*5*3*2*	L * L R	L R L *	L R L *	L L ^ *
1*5*2*3*	L * L R	L R L *	L L ^ *	L R L *
3*5*2*1*	L R L *	L R L R	L * L L	^ * L *
3*5*1*2*	L R L *	L R L *	L * L *	L L ^ *
3*1*2*5*	L R L *	L * L L	^ * L R	L R L *

SYNCOPATION

LESSON SIX
SYNCOPATED 2 BASICS LEFT

3-2-3-1-1 LEFT HAND

3*2*3*1*1*	L R L *	L L ^ *	L R L *	L * L *
3*2*1*3*1*	L R L *	L L ^ *	L * L R	L * L *
3*2*1*1*3*	L R L *	L L ^ *	L * L *	L R L *
3*3*1*1*2*	L R L *	L R L *	L * L *	L L ^ *
3*3*1*2*1*	L R L *	L R L *	L * L L	^ * L *
3*3*2*1*1*	L R L *	L R L *	L L ^ *	L * L *
2*3*3*1*1*	L L ^ *	L R L *	L R L *	L * L *
2*3*1*3*1*	L L ^ *	L R L *	L * L R	L * L *
2*3*1*1*3*	L L ^ *	L R L *	L * L *	L R L *
2*1*1*3*3*	L L ^ *	L * L *	L R L *	L R L *
2*1*3*1*3*	L L ^ *	L * L R	L * L *	L R L *
2*1*3*3*1*	L L ^ *	L * L R	L * L R	L * L *
1*2*3*3*1*	L * L L	^ * L R	L * L R	L * L *
1*2*3*1*3*	L * L L	^ * L R	L * L *	L R L *
1*2*1*3*3*	L * L L	^ * L *	L R L *	L R L *
1*1*3*3*2*	L * L *	L R L *	L R L *	L L ^ *
1*1*3*2*3*	L * L *	L R L *	L L ^ *	L R L *
1*1*2*3*3*	L * L *	L L ^ *	L R L *	L R L *
1*3*2*3*1*	L * L R	L * L L	^ * L R	L * L *
1*3*2*1*3*	L * L R	L * L L	^ * L *	L R L *
1*3*1*2*3*	L * L R	L * L *	L L ^ *	L R L *

SYNCOPATION

LESSON SIX
SYNCOPATED 2 BASICS LEFT

2-7-1-1 LEFT HAND

2*7*1*1*	L L ^ *	L R L R	L R L *	L * L *
2*1*7*1*	L L ^ *	L * L R	L R L R	L * L *
2*1*1*7*	L L ^ *	L * L *	L R L R	L R L *
7*1*1*2*	L R L R	L R L *	L * L *	L L ^ *
7*1*2*1*	L R L R	L R L *	L * L L	^ * L *
7*2*1*1*	L R L R	L R L *	L L ^ *	L * L *
2*7*1*1*	L L ^ *	L R L R	L R L *	L * L *
2*1*7*1*	L L ^ *	L * L R	L R L R	L * L *
2*1*1*7*	L L ^ *	L * L *	L R L R	L R L *

5-1-2-2 LEFT HAND

5*1*2*2*	L R L R	L * L *	L L ^ *	L L ^ *
5*2*1*2*	L R L R	L * L L	^ * L *	L L ^ *
5*2*2*1*	L R L R	L * L L	^ * L L	^ * L *
2*1*5*2*	L L ^ *	L * L R	L R L *	L L ^ *
2*1*2*5*	L L ^ *	L * L L	^ * L R	L R L *
2*5*2*1*	L L ^ *	L R L R	L * L L	^ * L *
2*5*1*2*	L L ^ *	L R L R	L * L *	L L ^ *
1*5*2*2*	L * L R	L R L *	L L ^ *	L L ^ *
1*2*5*2*	L * L L	^ * L R	L R L *	L L ^ *
1*2*2*5*	L * L L	^ * L L	^ * L R	L R L *

SYNCOPATION

LESSON SEVEN
SYNCOPATED 2 AND 4 BASICS RIGHT AND LEFT

SYNCOPATED 2 AND 4 BASICS RIGHT

2*4*5*	R R ^ *	R L ^ L	R * R L	R L R *

4*1*2*3*	R L ^ L	R * R *	R R ^ *	R L R *

4*2*2*1*	R L ^ L	R * R R	^ * R R	^ * R *

4*4*2*	R L ^ L	R * R L	^ L R *	R R ^ *

SYNCOPATED 2 AND 4 BASICS LEFT

2*4*5*	L L ^ *	L R ^ R	L * L R	L R L *

4*1*2*3*	L R ^ R	L * L *	L L ^ *	L R L *

4*2*2*1*	L R ^ R	L * L L	^ * L L	^ * L *

4*4*2*	L R ^ R	L * L R	^ R L *	L L ^ *

SYNCOPATION

LESSON EIGHT
SYNCOPATED 2 AND 4 RIGHT

2-4-5 RIGHT HAND

2*4*5*	R R ^ *	R L ^ L	R * R L	R L R *
2*5*4*	R R ^ *	R L R L	R * R L	^ L R *
4*2*5*	R L ^ L	R * R R	^ * R L	R L R *
4*5*2*	R L ^ L	R * R L	R L R *	R R ^ *
5*4*2*	R L R L	R * R L	^ L R *	R R ^ *
5*2*4*	R L R L	R * R R	^ * R L	^ L R *

4-4-2 RIGHT HAND

4*4*2*	R L ^ L	R * R L	^ L R *	R R ^ *
4*2*4*	R L ^ L	R * R R	^ * R L	^ L R *
2*4*4*	R R ^ *	R L ^ L	R * R L	^ L R *

4-2-2-1 RIGHT HAND

4*2*2*1*	R L ^ L	R * R R	^ * R R	^ * R *
4*1*2*2*	R L ^ L	R * R *	R R ^ *	R R ^ *
2*4*2*1*	R R ^ *	R L ^ L	R * R R	^ * R *
2*4*1*2*	R R ^ *	R L ^ L	R * R *	R R ^ *
2*1*4*2*	R R ^ *	R * R L	^ L R *	R R ^ *
1*2*4*2*	R * R R	^ * R L	^ L R *	R R ^ *
1*2*2*4*	R * R R	^ * R R	^ * R L	^ L R *
1*4*2*2*	R * R L	^ L R *	R R ^ *	R R ^ *

SYNCOPATION

LESSON EIGHT
SYNCOPATED 2 AND 4 RIGHT

4-1-2-3 RIGHT HAND

4*1*2*3*	R L ^ L	R * R *	R R ^ *	R L R *
4*1*3*2*	R L ^ L	R * R *	R L R *	R R ^ *
4*2*1*3*	R L ^ L	R * R R	^ * R *	R L R *
4*2*3*1*	R L ^ L	R * R R	^ * R L	R * R *
4*3*1*2*	R L ^ L	R * R L	R * R *	R R ^ *
4*3*2*1*	R L ^ L	R * R L	R * R R	^ * R *
3*1*2*4*	R L R *	R * R R	^ * R L	^ L R *
3*1*4*2*	R L R *	R * R L	^ L R *	R R ^ *
3*2*1*4*	R L R *	R R ^ *	R * R L	^ L R *
3*2*4*1*	R L R *	R R ^ *	R L ^ L	R * R *
3*4*1*2*	R L R *	R L ^ L	R * R *	R R ^ *
3*4*2*1*	R L R *	R L ^ L	R * R R	^ * R *
2*1*3*4*	R R ^ *	R * R L	R * R L	^ L R *
2*1*4*3*	R R ^ *	R * R L	^ L R *	R L R *
2*3*4*1*	R R ^ *	R L R *	R L ^ L	R * R *
2*3*1*4*	R R ^ *	R L R *	R * R L	^ L R *
1*2*3*4*	R * R R	^ * R L	R * R L	^ L R *
1*2*4*3*	R * R R	^ * R L	^ L R *	R L R *
1*3*2*4*	R * R L	R * R R	^ * R L	^ L R *

SYNCOPATION

LESSON NINE
SYNCOPATED 2 AND 4 LEFT

2-4-5 LEFT HAND

2*4*5*	L L ^ *	L R ^ R	L * L R	L R L *
2*5*4*	L L ^ *	L R L R	L * L R	^ R L *
4*2*5*	L R ^ R	L * L L	^ * L R	L R L *
4*5*2*	L R ^ R	L * L R	L R L *	L L ^ *
5*4*2*	L R L R	L * L R	^ R L *	L L ^ *
5*2*4*	L R L R	L * L L	^ * L R	^ R L *

4-4-2 LEFT HAND

4*4*2*	L R ^ R	L * L R	^ R L *	L L ^ *
4*2*4*	L R ^ R	L * L L	^ * L R	^ R L *
2*4*4*	L L ^ *	L R ^ R	L * L R	^ R L *

4-2-2-1 LEFT HAND

4*2*2*1*	L R ^ R	L * L L	^ * L L	^ * L *
4*1*2*2*	L R ^ R	L * L *	L L ^ *	L L ^ *
2*4*2*1*	L L ^ *	L R ^ R	L * L L	^ * L *
2*4*1*2*	L L ^ *	L R ^ R	L * L *	L L ^ *
2*1*4*2*	L L ^ *	L * L R	^ R L *	L L ^ *
1*2*4*2*	L * L L	^ * L R	^ R L *	L L ^ *
1*2*2*4*	L * L L	^ * L L	^ * L R	^ R L *
1*4*2*2*	L * L R	^ R L *	L L ^ *	L L ^ *

SYNCOPATION

LESSON NINE
SYNCOPATED 2 AND 4 LEFT

4-1-2-3 LEFT HAND

4*1*2*3*	L R ^ R	L * L *	L L ^ *	L R L *
4*1*3*2*	L R ^ R	L * L *	L R L *	L L ^ *
4*2*1*3*	L R ^ R	L * L L	^ * L *	L R L *
4*2*3*1*	L R ^ R	L * L L	^ * L R	L * L *
4*3*1*2*	L R ^ R	L * L R	L * L *	L L ^ *
4*3*2*1*	L R ^ R	L * L R	L * L L	^ * L *
3*1*2*4*	L R L *	L * L L	^ * L R	^ R L *
3*1*4*2*	L R L *	L * L R	^ R L *	L L ^ *
3*2*1*4*	L R L *	L L ^ *	L * L R	^ R L *
3*2*4*1*	L R L *	L L ^ *	L R ^ R	L * L *
3*4*1*2*	L R L *	L R ^ R	L * L *	L L ^ *
3*4*2*1*	L R L *	L R ^ R	L * L L	^ * L *
2*1*3*4*	L L ^ *	L * L R	L * L R	^ R L *
2*1*4*3*	L L ^ *	L * L R	^ R L *	L R L *
2*3*4*1*	L L ^ *	L R L *	L R ^ R	L * L *
2*3*1*4*	L L ^ *	L R L *	L * L R	^ R L *
1*2*3*4*	L * L L	^ * L R	L * L R	^ R L *
1*2*4*3*	L * L L	^ * L R	^ R L *	L R L *
1*3*2*4*	L * L R	L * L L	^ * L R	^ R L *

SECTION 5

TIMING VARIATION

TIMING VARIATION

INTRODUCTION TO TIMING VARIATION

Time signature is the measuring of beats within measures. The most common is 4/4 time in Western Pop music. Another common variation explored here is the Waltzy 6/8 time-signature. Basic factors are arranged into phrases equaling twenty-four beats.

TIME SIGNATURE

Time signature is an element of rhythm which effects the mood/feeling of the music. Beats are counted to fit into measures, creating a framework for numeric order, pattern prediction based on a fixed number of beats per measure.

STANDARD TIME SIGNATURE

Standard 4/4 Time signature- 4 beats per measure, a whole note is one beat.

TIMING VARIATIONS- 6 BEATS

Variation- 6/8 Time signature indicates 6 whole notes per measure.
This 6/8 timing creates a waltzing feeling, a subtle swing to the music.

> Variant 6/8 timing is found in many musical traditions
> > Classical music traditions
> > Persian traditional and modern music
> > African rhythms from several cultural groups

> Other Interesting time signatures to be considered, including
> > Turkish Karsilama inspired 9/8
> > Armenian inspired 10/8
> > Khaleegi inspired 5/4

TIMING VARIATION 6 BEAT LESSON BY LESSON
LESSON ONE- BASIC 6 BEAT FACTORS RIGHT AND LEFT
LESSON TWO- FACTOR BY FACTOR RIGHT AND LEFT
LESSON THREE- FACTOR COMBINATIONS RIGHT
LESSON FOUR- FACTOR COMBINATIONS LEFT

TIMING VARIATION

LESSON ONE
BASIC 6/8 FACTORS RIGHT AND LEFT

TIMING VARIATION 6 BEAT
BASIC PATTERNS RIGHT HAND

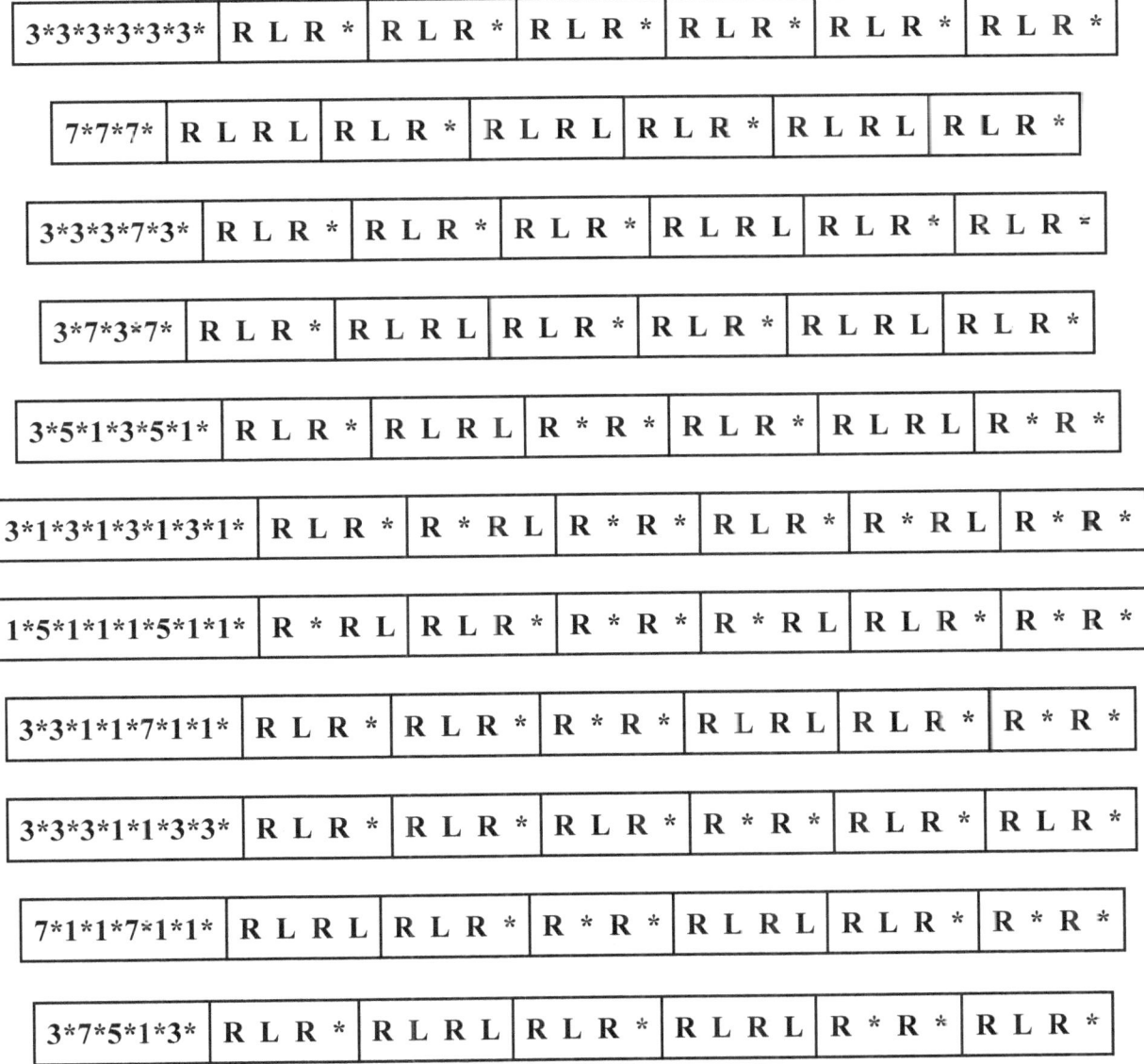

| 3*3*3*3*3*3* | R L R * | R L R * | R L R * | R L R * | R L R * | R L R * |

| 7*7*7* | R L R L | R L R * | R L R L | R L R * | R L R L | R L R * |

| 3*3*3*7*3* | R L R * | R L R * | R L R * | R L R L | R L R * | R L R * |

| 3*7*3*7* | R L R * | R L R L | R L R * | R L R * | R L R L | R L R * |

| 3*5*1*3*5*1* | R L R * | R L R L | R * R * | R L R * | R L R L | R * R * |

| 3*1*3*1*3*1*3*1* | R L R * | R * R L | R * R * | R L R * | R * R L | R * R * |

| 1*5*1*1*1*5*1*1* | R * R L | R L R * | R * R * | R * R L | R L R * | R * R * |

| 3*3*1*1*7*1*1* | R L R * | R L R * | R * R * | R L R L | R L R * | R * R * |

| 3*3*3*1*1*3*3* | R L R * | R L R * | R L R * | R * R * | R L R * | R L R * |

| 7*1*1*7*1*1* | R L R L | R L R * | R * R * | R L R L | R L R * | R * R * |

| 3*7*5*1*3* | R L R * | R L R L | R L R * | R L R L | R * R * | R L R * |

TIMING VARIATION

LESSON ONE
BASIC 6/8 FACTORS RIGHT AND LEFT

TIMING VARIATION 6 BEAT
BASIC PATTERNS RIGHT LEFT

| 3*3*3*3*3*3* | L R L * | L R L * | L R L * | L R L * | L R L * | L R L * |

| 7*7*7* | L R L R | L R L * | L R L R | L R L * | L R L R | L R L * |

| 3*3*3*7*3* | L R L * | L R L * | L R L * | L R L R | L R L * | L R L * |

| 3*7*3*7* | L R L * | L R L R | L R L * | L R L * | L R L R | L R L * |

| 3*5*1*3*5*1* | L R L * | L R L R | L * L * | L R L * | L R L R | L * L * |

| 3*1*3*1*3*1*3*1* | L R L * | L * L R | L * L * | L R L * | L * L R | L * L * |

| 1*5*1*1*1*5*1*1* | L * L R | L R L * | L * L * | L * L R | L R L * | L * L ** |

| 3*3*1*1*7*1*1* | L R L * | L R L * | L * L * | L R L R | L R L * | L * L * |

| 3*3*3*1*1*3*3* | L R L * | L R L * | L R L * | L * L * | L R L * | L R L * |

| 7*1*1*7*1*1* | L R L R | L R L * | L * L * | L R L R | L R L * | L * L * |

| 3*7*5*1*3* | L R L * | L R L R | L R L * | L R L R | L * L * | L R L * |

TIMING VARIATION

LESSON TWO
FACTOR BY FACTOR RIGHT

TIMING VARIATION 6 BEAT
BASIC 3's RIGHT HAND

3*3*3*3*3*3*	R L R *	R L R *	R L R *	R L R *	R L R *	R L R *

TIMING VARIATION 6 BEAT
BASIC 3's RIGHT HAND

7*7*7*	R L R L	R L R *	R L R L	R L R *	R L R L	R L R *

TIMING VARIATION 6 BEAT
3-3-3-7-3 RIGHT HAND

3*3*3*7*3*	R L R *	R L R *	R L R *	R L R L	R L R =	R L R *
3*3*7*3*3*	R L R *	R L R *	R L R L	R L R *	R L R =	R L R *
3*7*3*3*3*	R L R *	R L R L	R L R *	R L R *	R L R *	R L R *
7*3*3*3*3*	R L R L	R L R *	R L R *	R L R *	R L R *	R L R *
3*3*3*3*7	R L R *	R L R *	R L R *	R L R *	R L R L	R L R *

TIMING VARIATION 6 BEAT
3-7-3-7 RIGHT HAND

3*7*3*7*	R L R *	R L R L	R L R *	R L R *	R L R L	R L R *
3*7*7*3*	R L R *	R L R L	R L R *	R L R L	R L R *	R L R *
3*3*7*7*	R L R *	R L R *	R L R L	R L R *	R L R L	R L R *
7*3*7*3*	R L R L	R L R *	R L R *	R L R L	R L R *	R L R *
7*3*3*7*	R L R L	R L R *	R L R *	R L R *	R L R L	R L R *
7*7*3*3*	R L R L	R L R *	R L R L	R L R *	R L R *	R L R *

RHYTHM FACTORING

TIMING VARIATION

LESSON TWO
FACTOR BY FACTOR LEFT

TIMING VARIATION 6 BEAT
BASIC 3's LEFT HAND

3*3*3*3*3*3*	L R L *	L R L *	L R L *	L R L *	L R L *	L R L *

TIMING VARIATION 6 BEAT
BASIC 3's LEFT HAND

7*7*7*	L R L R	L R L *	L R L R	L R L *	L R L R	L R L *

TIMING VARIATION 6 BEAT
3-3-3-7-3 LEFT HAND

3*3*3*7*3*	L R L *	L R L *	L R L *	L R L R	L R L *	L R L *
3*3*7*3*3*	L R L *	L R L *	L R L R	L R L *	L R L *	L R L *
3*7*3*3*3*	L R L *	L R L R	L R L *	L R L *	L R L *	L R L *
7*3*3*3*3*	L R L R	L R L *	L R L *	L R L *	L R L *	L R L *
3*3*3*3*7*	L R L *	L R L *	L R L *	L R L *	L R L R	L R L *

TIMING VARIATION 6 BEAT
3-7-3-7 LEFT HAND

3*7*3*7*	L R L *	L R L R	L R L *	L R L *	L R L R	L R L *
3*7*7*3*	L R L *	L R L R	L R L *	L R L R	L R L *	L R L *
3*3*7*7*	L R L *	L R L *	L R L R	L R L *	L R L R	L R L *
7*3*7*3*	L R L R	L R L *	L R L *	L R L R	L R L *	L R L *
7*3*3*7*	L R L R	L R L *	L R L *	L R L *	L R L R	L R L *
7*7*3*3*	L R L R	L R L *	L R L R	L R L *	L R L *	L R L *

TIMING VARIATION

LESSON THREE
FACTOR COMBINATIONS RIGHT

TIMING VARIATION 6 BEAT
3-5-1-3-5-1 RIGHT HAND

3*5*1*3*1*5*	R L R *	R L R L	R * R *	R L R *	R * R L	R L R *
3*5*1*1*3*5*	R L R *	R L R L	R * R *	R * R L	R * R L	R L R *
3*5*1*1*5*3*	R L R *	R L R L	R * R *	R * R L	R L R *	R L R *
3*1*5*1*3*5*	R L R *	R * R L	R L R *	R * R L	R * R L	R L R *
3*1*5*1*5*3*	R L R *	R * R L	R L R *	R * R L	R L R *	R L R *
3*1*5*3*1*5*	R L R *	R * R L	R L R *	R L R *	R * R L	R L R *
3*1*5*3*5*1*	R L R *	R * R L	R L R *	R L R *	R L R L	R * R *
3*1*5*5*3*1*	R L R *	R * R L	R L R *	R L R L	R * R L	R * R *
3*1*5*5*1*3*	R L R *	R * R L	R L R *	R L R L	R * R *	R L R *
3*1*5*3*5*1*	R L R *	R * R L	R L R *	R L R *	R L R L	R * R *
3*1*5*5*3*1*	R L R *	R * R L	R L R *	R L R L	R * R L	R * R *
3*1*5*5*1*3*	R L R *	R * R L	R L R *	R L R L	R * R *	R L R *
3*5*1*5*3*1*	R L R *	R L R L	R * R *	R L R L	R * R L	R * R *
3*5*1*5*1*3*	R L R *	R L R L	R * R *	R L R L	R * R *	R L R *
3*5*1*3*5*1*	R L R *	R L R L	R * R *	R L R *	R L R L	R * R *
3*5*1*3*1*5*	R L R *	R L R L	R * R *	R L R *	R * R L	R L R *
3*5*5*1*3*1*	R L R *	R L R L	R * R L	R L R *	R * R L	R * R *
3*5*5*1*1*3*	R L R *	R L R L	R * R L	R L R *	R * R *	R L R *
3*5*5*3*1*1*	R L R *	R L R L	R * R L	R L R *	R L R *	R * R *
3*3*5*5*1*1*	R L R *	R L R *	R L R L	R * R L	R L R *	R * R *

TIMING VARIATION

LESSON THREE
FACTOR COMBINATIONS RIGHT

TIMING VARIATION 6 BEAT
3-1-3-1-3-1-3-1   RIGHT HAND

3*1*3*1*3*1*3*1	R L R *	R * R L	R * R *	R L R *	R * R L	R * R *
3*1*3*1*3*1*1*3	R L R *	R * R L	R * R *	R L R *	R * R *	R L R *
3*1*3*1*3*3*1*1	R L R *	R * R L	R * R *	R L R *	R L R *	R * R *
3*1*3*1*1*3*1*3	R L R *	R * R L	R * R *	R * R L	R * R *	R L R *
3*1*3*3*1*3*1*1	R L R *	R * R L	R * R L	R * R *	R L R *	R * R *
3*1*3*3*1*1*3*1	R L R *	R * R L	R * R L	R * R *	R * R L	R * R *
3*1*3*3*1*1*1*3	R L R *	R * R L	R * R L	R * R *	R * R *	R L R *
3*1*3*3*3*1*1*1	R L R *	R * R L	R * R L	R * R L	R * R *	R * R *
3*1*1*3*1*3*1*3	R L R *	R * R *	R L R *	R * R L	R * R *	R L R *
3*1*1*3*1*1*3*3	R L R *	R * R *	R L R *	R * R *	R L R *	R L R *
3*1*1*3*3*1*1*3	R L R *	R * R *	R L R *	R L R *	R * R *	R L R *
3*1*1*3*3*3*1*1	R L R *	R * R *	R L R *	R L R *	R L R *	R * R *
3*3*1*3*1*3*1*1	R L R *	R L R *	R * R L	R * R *	R L R *	R * R *
3*3*1*3*1*1*3*1	R L R *	R L R *	R * R L	R * R *	R * R L	R * R *
3*3*1*3*3*1*1*1	R L R *	R L R *	R * R L	R * R L	R * R *	R * R *
3*3*1*1*3*1*3*1	R L R *	R L R *	R * R *	R L R *	R * R L	R * R *
3*3*1*1*3*1*1*3	R L R *	R L R *	R * R *	R L R *	R * R *	R L R *
3*3*1*1*1*3*1*3	R L R *	R L R *	R * R *	R * R L	R * R *	R L R *
3*3*3*1*1*1*3*1	R L R *	R L R *	R L R *	R * R *	R * R L	R * R *
3*3*1*1*1*1*3*3	R L R *	R L R *	R * R *	R * R *	R L R *	R L R *

TIMING VARIATION

LESSON THREE
FACTOR COMBINATIONS RIGHT

TIMING VARIATION 6 BEAT
1-5-1-1-1-5-1-1   RIGHT HAND

1*5*1*1*1*5*1*1	R * R L	R L R *	R * R *	R * R L	R L R *	R * R *
1*5*1*1*1*1*5*1	R * R L	R L R *	R * R *	R * R *	R L R L	R * R *
1*5*1*1*1*1*1*5	R * R L	R L R *	R * R *	R * R *	R * R L	R L R *
1*5*1*1*5*1*1*1	R * R L	R L R *	R * R *	R L R L	R * R *	R * R *
1*5*1*5*1*1*1*1	R * R L	R L R *	R * R L	R L R *	R * R *	R * R *
1*5*5*1*1*1*1*1	R * R L	R L R *	R L R L	R * R	R * R *	R * R *
1*1*5*5*1*1*1*1	R * R *	R L R L	R * R L	R L R *	R * R *	R * R *
1*1*5*1*5*1*1*1	R * R *	R L R L	R * R *	R L R L	R * R *	R * R *
1*1*5*1*1*5*1*1	R * R *	R L R L	R * R *	R * R L	R L R *	R * R *
1*1*5*1*1*1*5*1	R * R *	R L R L	R * R *	R * R *	R L R L	R * R *
1*1*5*1*1*1*1*5	R * R *	R L R L	R * R *	R * R *	R * R L	R L R *
1*1*1*5*5*1*1*1	R * R *	R * R L	R L R *	R L R L	R * R *	R * R *
1*1*1*5*1*5*1*1	R * R *	R * R L	R L R *	R * R L	R L R *	R * R *
1*1*1*5*1*1*5*1	R * R *	R * R L	R L R *	R * R *	R L R L	R * R *
1*1*1*5*1*1*1*5	R * R *	R * R L	R L R *	R * R *	R * R L	R L R *
1*1*1*1*5*5*1*1	R * R *	R * R *	R L R L	R * R L	R L R *	R * R *
1*1*1*1*5*1*5*1	R * R *	R * R *	R L R L	R * R *	R L R L	R * R *
1*1*1*1*1*5*5*1	R * R *	R * R *	R * R L	R L R *	R L R L	R * R *
1*1*1*1*1*5*1*5	R * R *	R * R *	R * R L	R L R *	R * R L	R L R *
1*1*1*1*1*1*5*5	R * R *	R * R *	R * R *	R L R L	R * R L	R L R *

TIMING VARIATION

LESSON THREE
FACTOR COMBINATIONS RIGHT

TIMING VARIATION 6 BEAT
3-3-1-1-7-1-1 RIGHT HAND

3*3*1*1*7*1*1*	R L R *	R L R *	R * R *	R L R L	R L R *	R * R *
3*3*1*7*1*1*1*	R L R *	R L R *	R * R L	R L R L	R * R *	R * R *
3*3*7*1*1*1*1*	R L R *	R L R *	R L R L	R L R *	R * R *	R * R *
3*7*3*1*1*1*1*	R L R *	R L R L	R L R *	R L R *	R * R *	R * R *
3*3*1*1*1*7*1*	R L R *	R L R *	R * R *	R * R L	R L R L	R * R *
3*3*1*1*1*1*7	R L R *	R L R *	R * R *	R * R *	R L R L	R L R *
3*7*1*3*1*1*1*	R L R *	R L R L	R L R *	R * R L	R * R *	R * R *
3*7*1*1*3*1*1*	R L R *	R L R L	R L R *	R * R *	R L R *	R * R *
3*7*1*1*1*3*1*	R L R *	R L R L	R L R *	R * R *	R * R L	R * R *
3*7*1*1*1*1*3*	R L R *	R L R L	R L R *	R * R *	R * R *	R L R *
3*1*3*1*1*7*1*	R L R *	R * R L	R * R *	R * R L	R L R L	R * R *
3*1*3*1*1*1*7	R L R *	R * R L	R * R *	R * R *	R L R L	R L R *
3*1*3*1*7*1*1*	R L R *	R * R L	R * R *	R L R L	R L R *	R * R *
3*1*3*7*1*1*1*	R L R *	R * R L	R * R L	R L R L	R * R *	R * R *
3*1*1*3*7*1*1*	R L R *	R * R *	R L R *	R L R L	R L R *	R * R *
3*1*1*3*1*7*1*	R L R *	R * R *	R L R *	R * R L	R L R L	R * R *
3*1*1*3*1*1*7	R L R *	R * R *	R L R *	R * R *	R L R L	R L R *
3*1*1*1*3*1*7	R L R *	R * R *	R * R L	R * R *	R L R L	R L R *
3*1*1*1*3*7*1*	R L R *	R * R *	R * R L	R * R L	R L R L	R * R *
3*1*1*1*1*3*7*	R L R *	R * R *	R * R *	R L R *	R L R L	R L R *

TIMING VARIATION

LESSON THREE
FACTOR COMBINATIONS RIGHT

TIMING VARIATION 6 BEAT
3-3-3-1-1-3-3 RIGHT HAND

3*3*3*1*1*3*3*	R L R *	R L R *	R L R *	R * R *	R L R *	R L R *
3*3*3*1*3*1*3*	R L R *	R L R *	R L R *	R * R L	R * R *	R L R *
3*3*3*1*3*3*1*	R L R *	R L R *	R L R *	R * R L	R * R L	R * R *
3*3*1*3*1*3*3*	R L R *	R L R *	R * R L	R * R *	R L R *	R L R *
3*3*1*3*3*3*1*	R L R *	R L R *	R * R L	R * R L	R * R L	R * R *
3*3*1*1*3*3*3*	R L R *	R L R *	R * R *	R L R *	R L R *	R L R *
3*1*1*3*3*3*3*	R L R *	R * R *	R L R *	R L R *	R L R *	R L R *
3*3*3*3*3*1*1*	R L R *	R L R *	R L R *	R L R *	R L R *	R * R *
3*3*3*3*1*1*3*	R L R *	R L R *	R L R *	R L R *	R * R *	R L R *
3*3*3*3*1*3*1*	R L R *	R L R *	R L R *	R L R *	R * R L	R * R *
3*1*3*1*3*3*3*	R L R *	R * R L	R * R *	R L R *	R L R *	R L R *
3*1*3*3*3*3*1*	R L R *	R * R L	R * R L	R * R L	R * R L	R * R *
3*1*3*3*3*1*3*	R L R *	R * R L	R * R L	R * R L	R * R *	R L R *
3*1*3*3*1*3*3*	R L R *	R * R L	R * R L	R * R *	R L R *	R L R *
3*3*1*3*3*1*3*	R L R *	R L R *	R * R L	R * R L	R * R *	R L R *
1*3*1*3*3*3*3*	R * R L	R * R *	R L R *	R L R *	R L R *	R L R *
1*3*3*1*3*3*3*	R * R L	R * R L	R * R *	R L R *	R L R *	R L R *
1*3*3*3*1*3*3*	R * R L	R * R L	R * R L	R * R *	R L R *	R L R *
1*3*3*3*3*1*3*	R * R L	R * R L	R * R L	R * R L	R * R *	R L R *
1*3*3*3*3*3*1*	R * R L	R * R L	R * R L	R * R L	R * R L	R * R *

TIMING VARIATION

LESSON THREE
FACTOR COMBINATIONS RIGHT

TIMING VARIATION 6 BEAT
7-1-1-7-1-1 RIGHT HAND

7*1*1*7*1*1*	R L R L	R L R *	R * R *	R L R L	R L R *	R * R *
7*1*1*1*1*7*	R L R L	R L R *	R * R *	R * R *	R L R L	R L R *
7*1*1*1*7*1*	R L R L	R L R *	R * R *	R * R L	R L R L	R * R *
7*1*7*1*1*1*	R L R L	R L R *	R * R L	R L R L	R * R *	R * R *
7*7*1*1*1*1*	R L R L	R L R *	R L R L	R L R *	R * R *	R * R *
1*7*1*1*1*7*	R * R L	R L R L	R * R *	R * R *	R L R L	R L R *
1*7*1*1*7*1*	R * R L	R L R L	R * R *	R * R L	R L R L	R * R *
1*7*1*7*1*1*	R * R L	R L R L	R * R *	R L R L	R L R *	R * R *
1*7*7*1*1*1*	R * R L	R L R L	R * R L	R L R L	R * R *	R * R *
1*1*7*1*1*7*	R * R *	R L R L	R L R *	R * R *	R L R L	R L R *
1*1*7*1*7*1*	R * R *	R L R L	R L R *	R * R L	R L R L	R * R *
1*1*7*7*1*1*	R * R *	R L R L	R L R *	R L R L	R L R *	R * R *
1*1*1*7*1*7*	R * R *	R * R L	R L R L	R * R *	R L R L	R L R *
1*1*1*7*7*1*	R * R *	R * R L	R L R L	R * R L	R L R L	R * R *
1*1*1*1*7*7*	R * R *	R * R *	R L R L	R L R *	R L R L	R L R *

TIMING VARIATION

LESSON THREE
FACTOR COMBINATIONS RIGHT

TIMING VARIATION 6 BEAT
3-7-5-1-3 RIGHT HAND

3*7*5*1*3*	R L R *	R L R L	R L R *	R L R L	R * R *	R L R *
3*7*5*3*1*	R L R *	R L R L	R L R *	R L R L	R * R L	R * R *
3*7*1*5*3*	R L R *	R L R L	R L R *	R * R L	R L R *	R L R *
3*7*1*3*5*	R L R *	R L R L	R L R *	R * R L	R * R L	R L R *
3*7*3*1*5*	R L R *	R L R L	R L R *	R L R *	R * R L	R L R *
3*7*5*3*1*	R L R *	R L R L	R L R *	R L R L	R * R L	R * R *
7*3*5*3*1*	R L R L	R L R *	R L R *	R L R L	R * R L	R * R *
7*3*5*1*3*	R L R L	R L R *	R L R *	R L R L	R * R *	R L R *
7*3*3*5*1*	R L R L	R L R *	R L R *	R L R *	R L R L	R * R *
7*3*3*1*5*	R L R L	R L R *	R L R *	R L R *	R * R L	R L R *
7*3*1*5*3*	R L R L	R L R *	R L R *	R * R L	R L R *	R L R *
7*3*1*3*5*	R L R L	R L R *	R L R *	R * R L	R * R L	R L R *
5*7*3*1*3*	R L R L	R * R L	R L R L	R * R L	R * R *	R L R *
5*7*3*3*1*	R L R L	R * R L	R L R L	R * R L	R * R L	R * R *
5*7*1*3*3*	R L R L	R * R L	R L R L	R * R *	R L R *	R L R *
5*3*1*3*7*	R L R L	R * R L	R * R *	R L R *	R L R L	R L R *
5*1*3*7*3*	R L R L	R * R *	R L R *	R L R L	R L R *	R L R =
5*1*3*3*7*	R L R L	R * R *	R L R *	R L R *	R L R L	R L R *
5*1*7*3*3*	R L R L	R * R *	R L R L	R L R *	R L R *	R L R *
5*3*7*3*1*	R L R L	R * R L	R * R L	R L R L	R * R L	R * R *

TIMING VARIATION

LESSON FOUR
FACTOR COMBINATIONS LEFT

TIMING VARIATION 6 BEAT
3-5-1-3-5-1 LEFT HAND

3*5*1*3*1*5*	L R L *	L R L R	L * L *	L R L *	L * L R	L R L *
3*5*1*1*3*5*	L R L *	L R L R	L * L *	L * L R	L * L R	L R L *
3*5*1*1*5*3*	L R L *	L R L R	L * L *	L * L R	L R L *	L R L *
3*1*5*1*3*5*	L R L *	L * L R	L R L *	L * L R	L * L R	L R L *
3*1*5*1*5*3*	L R L *	L * L R	L R L *	L * L R	L R L *	L R L *
3*1*5*3*1*5*	L R L *	L * L R	L R L *	L R L *	L * L R	L R L *
3*1*5*3*5*1*	L R L *	L * L R	L R L *	L R L *	L R L R	L * L *
3*1*5*5*3*1*	L R L *	L * L R	L R L *	L R L R	L * L R	L * L *
3*1*5*5*1*3*	L R L *	L * L R	L R L *	L R L R	L * L *	L R L *
3*1*5*3*5*1*	L R L *	L * L R	L R L *	L R L *	L R L R	L * L *
3*1*5*5*3*1*	L R L *	L * L R	L R L *	L R L R	L * L R	L * L *
3*1*5*5*1*3*	L R L *	L * L R	L R L *	L R L R	L * L *	L R L *
3*5*1*5*3*1*	L R L *	L R L R	L * L *	L R L R	L * L R	L * L *
3*5*1*5*1*3*	L R L *	L R L R	L * L *	L R L R	L * L *	L R L *
3*5*1*3*5*1*	L R L *	L R L R	L * L *	L R L *	L R L R	L * L *
3*5*1*3*1*5*	L R L *	L R L R	L * L *	L R L *	L * L R	L R L *
3*5*5*1*3*1*	L R L *	L R L R	L * L R	L R L *	L * L R	L * L *
3*5*5*1*1*3*	L R L *	L R L R	L * L R	L R L *	L * L *	L R L *
3*5*5*3*1*1*	L R L *	L R L R	L * L R	L R L *	L R L *	L * L *
3*3*5*5*1*1*	L R L *	L R L *	L R L R	L * L R	L R L *	L * L *

RHYTHM FACTORING

TIMING VARIATION

LESSON THREE
FACTOR COMBINATIONS RIGHT

TIMING VARIATION 6 BEAT
3-1-3-1-3-1-3-1 LEFT HAND

3*1*3*1*3*1*3*1	L R L *	L * L R	L * L *	L R L *	L * L R	L * L *
3*1*3*1*3*1*1*3	L R L *	L * L R	L * L *	L R L *	L * L *	L R L *
3*1*3*1*3*3*1*1	L R L *	L * L R	L * L *	L R L *	L R L *	L * L *
3*1*3*1*1*3*1*3	L R L *	L * L R	L * L *	L * L R	L * L *	L R L *
3*1*3*3*1*3*1*1	L R L *	L * L R	L * L R	L * L *	L R L *	L * L *
3*1*3*3*1*1*3*1	L R L *	L * L R	L * L R	L * L *	L * L R	L * L *
3*1*3*3*1*1*1*3	L R L *	L * L R	L * L R	L * L *	L * L *	L R L *
3*1*3*3*3*1*1*1	L R L *	L * L R	L * L R	L * L R	L * L *	L * L *
3*1*1*3*1*3*1*3	L R L *	L * L *	L R L *	L * L R	L * L *	L R L *
3*1*1*3*1*1*3*3	L R L *	L * L *	L R L *	L * L *	L R L *	L R L *
3*1*1*3*3*1*1*3	L R L *	L * L *	L R L *	L R L *	L * L *	L R L *
3*1*1*3*3*3*1*1	L R L *	L * L *	L R L *	L R L *	L R L *	L * L *
3*3*1*3*1*3*1*1	L R L *	L R L *	L * L R	L * L *	L R L *	L * L *
3*3*1*3*1*1*3*1	L R L *	L R L *	L * L R	L * L *	L * L R	L * L *
3*3*1*3*3*1*1*1	L R L *	L R L *	L * L R	L * L R	L * L *	L * L *
3*3*1*1*3*1*3*1	L R L *	L R L *	L * L *	L R L *	L * L R	L * L *
3*3*1*1*3*1*1*3	L R L *	L R L *	L * L *	L R L *	L * L *	L R L *
3*3*1*1*1*3*1*3	L R L *	L R L *	L * L *	L * L R	L * L *	L R L *
3*3*3*1*1*1*3*1	L R L *	L R L *	L R L *	L * L *	L * L R	L * L *
3*3*1*1*1*1*3*3	L R L *	L R L *	L * L *	L * L *	L R L *	L R L *

TIMING VARIATION

LESSON THREE
FACTOR COMBINATIONS RIGHT

TIMING VARIATION 6 BEAT
1-5-1-1-1-5-1-1 LEFT HAND

1*5*1*1*1*5*1*1	L * L R	L R L *	L * L *	L * L R	L R L *	L * L *
1*5*1*1*1*1*5*1	L * L R	L R L *	L * L *	L * L *	L R L R	L * L *
1*5*1*1*1*1*1*5	L * L R	L R L *	L * L *	L * L *	L * L R	L R L *
1*5*1*1*5*1*1*1	L * L R	L R L *	L * L *	L R L R	L * L *	L * L *
1*5*1*5*1*1*1*1	L * L R	L R L *	L * L R	L R L *	L * L *	L * L *
1*5*5*1*1*1*1*1	L * L R	L R L *	L R L R	L * L *	L * L *	L * L *
1*1*5*5*1*1*1*1	L * L *	L R L R	L * L R	L R L *	L * L *	L * L *
1*1*5*1*5*1*1*1	L * L *	L R L R	L * L *	L R L R	L * L *	L * L *
1*1*5*1*1*5*1*1	L * L *	L R L R	L * L *	L * L R	L R L *	L * L *
1*1*5*1*1*1*5*1	L * L *	L R L R	L * L *	L * L *	L R L R	L * L *
1*1*5*1*1*1*1*5	L * L *	L R L R	L * L *	L * L *	L * L R	L R L *
1*1*1*5*5*1*1*1	L * L *	L * L R	L R L *	L R L R	L * L *	L * L *
1*1*1*5*1*5*1*1	L * L *	L * L R	L R L *	L * L R	L R L *	L * L *
1*1*1*5*1*1*5*1	L * L *	L * L R	L R L *	L * L *	L R L R	L * L *
1*1*1*5*1*1*1*5	L * L *	L * L R	L R L *	L * L *	L * L R	L R L *
1*1*1*1*5*5*1*1	L * L *	L * L *	L R L R	L * L R	L R L *	L * L *
1*1*1*1*5*1*5*1	L * L *	L * L *	L R L R	L * L *	L R L R	L * L *
1*1*1*1*1*5*5*1	L * L *	L * L *	L * L R	L R L *	L R L R	L * L *
1*1*1*1*1*5*1*5	L * L *	L * L *	L * L R	L R L *	L * L R	L R L *
1*1*1*1*1*1*5*5	L * L *	L * L *	L * L *	L R L R	L * L R	L R L *

TIMING VARIATION

LESSON THREE
FACTOR COMBINATIONS RIGHT

TIMING VARIATION 6 BEAT
3-3-1-1-7-1-1 LEFT HAND

3*3*1*1*7*1*1*	L R L *	L R L *	L * L *	L R L R	L R L *	L * L *
3*3*1*7*1*1*1*	L R L *	L R L *	L * L R	L R L R	L * L *	L * L *
3*3*7*1*1*1*1*	L R L *	L R L *	L R L R	L R L *	L * L *	L * L *
3*7*3*1*1*1*1*	L R L *	L R L R	L R L *	L R L *	L * L *	L * L *
3*3*1*1*1*7*1*	L R L *	L R L *	L * L *	L * L R	L R L R	L * L *
3*3*1*1*1*1*7*	L R L *	L R L *	L * L *	L * L *	L R L R	L R L *
3*7*1*3*1*1*1*	L R L *	L R L R	L R L *	L * L R	L * L *	L * L *
3*7*1*1*3*1*1*	L R L *	L R L R	L R L *	L * L *	L R L *	L * L *
3*7*1*1*1*3*1*	L R L *	L R L R	L R L *	L * L *	L * L R	L * L *
3*7*1*1*1*1*3*	L R L *	L R L R	L R L *	L * L *	L * L *	L R L *
3*1*3*1*1*7*1*	L R L *	L * L R	L * L *	L * L R	L R L R	L * L *
3*1*3*1*1*1*7*	L R L *	L * L R	L * L *	L * L *	L R L R	L R L *
3*1*3*1*7*1*1*	L R L *	L * L R	L * L *	L R L R	L R L *	L * L *
3*1*3*7*1*1*1*	L R L *	L * L R	L * L R	L R L R	L * L *	L * L *
3*1*1*3*7*1*1*	L R L *	L * L *	L R L *	L R L R	L R L *	L * L *
3*1*1*3*1*7*1*	L R L *	L * L *	L R L *	L * L R	L R L R	L * L *
3*1*1*3*1*1*7*	L R L *	L * L *	L R L *	L * L *	L R L R	L R L *
3*1*1*1*3*1*7*	L R L *	L * L *	L * L R	L * L *	L R L R	L R L *
3*1*1*1*3*7*1*	L R L *	L * L *	L * L R	L * L R	L R L R	L * L *
3*1*1*1*1*3*7*	L R L *	L * L *	L * L *	L R L *	L R L R	L R L *

TIMING VARIATION

LESSON THREE
FACTOR COMBINATIONS RIGHT

TIMING VARIATION 6 BEAT
3-3-3-1-1-3-3 LEFT HAND

3*3*3*1*1*3*3*	L R L *	L R L *	L R L *	L * L *	L R L *	L R L *
3*3*3*1*3*1*3*	L R L *	L R L *	L R L *	L * L R	L * L *	L R L *
3*3*3*1*3*3*1*	L R L *	L R L *	L R L *	L * L R	L * L R	L * L *
3*3*1*3*1*3*3*	L R L *	L R L *	L * L R	L * L *	L R L *	L R L *
3*3*1*3*3*3*1*	L R L *	L R L *	L * L R	L * L R	L * L R	L * L *
3*3*1*1*3*3*3*	L R L *	L R L *	L * L *	L R L *	L R L *	L R L *
3*1*1*3*3*3*3*	L R L *	L * L *	L R L *	L R L *	L R L *	L R L *
3*3*3*3*3*1*1*	L R L *	L R L *	L R L *	L R L *	L R L *	L * L *
3*3*3*3*1*1*3*	L R L *	L R L *	L R L *	L R L *	L * L *	L R L *
3*3*3*3*1*3*1*	L R L *	L R L *	L R L *	L R L *	L * L R	L * L *
3*1*3*1*3*3*3*	L R L *	L * L R	L * L *	L R L *	L R L *	L R L *
3*1*3*3*3*3*1*	L R L *	L * L R	L * L R	L * L R	L * L R	L * L *
3*1*3*3*3*1*3*	L R L *	L * L R	L * L R	L * L R	L * L *	L R L *
3*1*3*3*1*3*3*	L R L *	L * L R	L * L R	L * L *	L R L *	L R L *
3*3*1*3*3*1*3*	L R L *	L R L *	L * L R	L * L R	L * L *	L R L *
1*3*1*3*3*3*3*	L * L R	L * L *	L R L *	L R L *	L R L *	L R L *
1*3*3*1*3*3*3*	L * L R	L * L R	L * L *	L R L *	L R L *	L R L *
1*3*3*3*1*3*3*	L * L R	L * L R	L * L R	L * L *	L R L *	L R L *
1*3*3*3*3*1*3*	L * L R	L * L R	L * L R	L * L R	L * L *	L R L *
1*3*3*3*3*3*1*	L * L R	L * L R	L * L R	L * L R	L * L R	L * L *

RHYTHM FACTORING

TIMING VARIATION

LESSON THREE
FACTOR COMBINATIONS RIGHT

TIMING VARIATION 6 BEAT
7-1-1-7-1-1 LEFT HAND

7*1*1*7*1*1*	L R L R	L R L *	L * L *	L R L R	L R L *	L * L *
7*1*1*1*1*7*	L R L R	L R L *	L * L *	L * L *	L R L R	L R L *
7*1*1*1*7*1*	L R L R	L R L *	L * L *	L * L R	L R L R	L * L *
7*1*7*1*1*1*	L R L R	L R L *	L * L R	L R L R	L * L *	L * L *
7*7*1*1*1*1*	L R L R	L R L *	L R L R	L R L *	L * L *	L * L *
1*7*1*1*1*7*	L * L R	L R L R	L * L *	L * L *	L R L R	L R L *
1*7*1*1*7*1*	L * L R	L R L R	L * L *	L * L R	L R L R	L * L *
1*7*1*7*1*1*	L * L R	L R L R	L * L *	L R L R	L R L *	L * L *
1*7*7*1*1*1*	L * L R	L R L R	L * L R	L R L R	L * L *	L * L *
1*1*7*1*1*7*	L * L *	L R L R	L R L *	L * L *	L R L R	L R L *
1*1*7*1*7*1*	L * L *	L R L R	L R L *	L * L R	L R L R	L * L *
1*1*7*7*1*1*	L * L *	L R L R	L R L *	L R L R	L R L *	L * L *
1*1*1*7*1*7*	L * L *	L * L R	L R L R	L * L *	L R L R	L R L *
1*1*1*7*7*1*	L * L *	L * L R	L R L R	L * L R	L R L R	L * L *
1*1*1*1*7*7*	L * L *	L * L *	L R L R	L R L *	L R L R	L R L *

TIMING VARIATION

LESSON THREE
FACTOR COMBINATIONS RIGHT

TIMING VARIATION 6 BEAT
3-7-5-1-3 LEFT HAND

3*7*5*1*3*	L R L *	L R L R	L R L *	L R L R	L * L *	L R L *
3*7*5*3*1*	L R L *	L R L R	L R L *	L R L R	L * L R	L * L *
3*7*1*5*3*	L R L *	L R L R	L R L *	L * L R	L R L *	L R L *
3*7*1*3*5*	L R L *	L R L R	L R L *	L * L R	L * L R	L R L *
3*7*3*1*5*	L R L *	L R L R	L R L *	L R L *	L * L R	L R L *
3*7*5*3*1*	L R L *	L R L R	L R L *	L R L R	L * L R	L * L *
7*3*5*3*1*	L R L R	L R L *	L R L *	L R L R	L * L R	L * L *
7*3*5*1*3*	L R L R	L R L *	L R L *	L R L R	L * L *	L R L *
7*3*3*5*1*	L R L R	L R L *	L R L *	L R L *	L R L R	L * L *
7*3*3*1*5*	L R L R	L R L *	L R L *	L R L *	L * L R	L R L *
7*3*1*5*3*	L R L R	L R L *	L R L *	L * L R	L R L *	L R L *
7*3*1*3*5*	L R L R	L R L *	L R L *	L * L R	L * L R	L R L *
5*7*3*1*3*	L R L R	L * L R	L R L R	L * L R	L * L *	L R L *
5*7*3*3*1*	L R L R	L * L R	L R L R	L * L R	L * L R	L * L *
5*7*1*3*3*	L R L R	L * L R	L R L R	L * L *	L R L *	L R L *
5*3*1*3*7*	L R L R	L * L R	L * L *	L R L *	L R L R	L R L *
5*1*3*7*3*	L R L R	L * L *	L R L *	L R L R	L R L *	L R L *
5*1*3*3*7*	L R L R	L * L *	L R L *	L R L *	L R L R	L R L *
5*1*7*3*3*	L R L R	L * L *	L R L R	L R L *	L R L *	L R L *
5*3*7*3*1*	L R L R	L * L R	L * L R	L R L R	L * L R	L * L *

SECTION 6

BIMANUAL DEXTERITY

BIMANUAL DEXTERITY

INTRODUCTION TO BIMANUAL DEXTERITY

Handedness, the concept of hand dominance is widespread. Both hands can develop competence, simple tasks can be done with either hand. Symmetrical competence is ability developed equally with both hands. Practice can correct extreme handedness, to develop balance and symmetry Drills and exercises help develop muscle memory of each hand Hand-eye coordination cultivated for both dominant and non-dominant hands. Develop the ability to play hand drums- shift toward ambidextrous capabilities.

LINE BY LINE TABLES

Rhythm patterns are organized in integrated pairings. Each table incorporates both right-hand lead and left-hand lead one line at a time. First line is right hand lead of the first factor pattern Second line is left hand lead of the same factor pattern. Each table contains twice as many lines as in previous section, contain both right and left-hand options together. By practicing each pattern first right then left, the muscle memory and hand-eye coordination needed to recognize these quick switches can increase tremendously with just a little practice.

FACTOR BY FACTOR TABLES

Rhythm Patterns are organized in continuous integration stream. Each table incorporates right and left-hand lead, one factor at a time. The first factor is a right-hand lead, second factor is left hand lead. Each pattern contains both right-hand factors and left-hand factors Each line is a blend of right and left-hand leads.

DEXTERITY PRACTICE LESSON BY LESSON

LESSON ONE- Basics Line by Line Right and Left
LESSON TWO- Basics Factor by Factor Right and Left

BIMANUAL DEXTERITY

LESSON ONE
BASICS LINE BY LINE RIGHT AND LEFT

R- 3*3*7*	R L R *	R L R *	R L R L	R L R *
L--3*3*7*	L R L *	L R L *	L R L R	L R L *

R- 3*5*5*	R L R *	R L R L	R * R L	R L R *
L- 3*5*5*	L R L *	L R L R	L * L R	L R L *

R- 7*7*	R L R L	R L R *	R L R L	R L R *
L- 7*7*	L R L R	L R L *	L R L R	L R L *

R- 3*1*3*1*3*	R L R *	R * R L	R * R *	R L R *
L- 3*1*3*1*3*	L R L *	L * L R	L * L *	L R L *

R- 5*1*5*1*	R L R L	R * R *	R L R L	R * R *
L- 5*1*5*1*	L R L R	L * L *	L R L R	L * L *

R- 3*5*1*3*	R L R *	R L R L	R * R *	R L R *
L- 3*5*1*3*	L R L *	L R L R	L * L *	L R L *

R- 3*1*7*1*	R L R *	R * R L	R L R L	R * R *
L- 3*1*7*1*	L R L *	L * L R	L R L R	L * L *

R- 3*1*1*5*1*	R L R *	R * R *	R L R L	R * R *
L- 3*1*1*5*1*	L R L *	L * L *	L R L R	L * L *

R—7*1*5*	R L R L	R L R *	R * R L	R L R *
L--7*1*5*	L R L R	L R L *	L * L R	L R L *

BIMANUAL DEXTERITY

LESSON ONE
BASICS LINE BY LINE RIGHT AND LEFT

3-3-7

R- 3*3*7*	R L R *	R L R *	R L R L	R L R *
L- 3*3*7*	L R L *	L R L *	L R L R	L R L *
R- 3*7*3*	R L R *	R L R L	R L R *	R L R *
L- 3*7*3*	L R L *	L R L R	L R L *	L R L *
R- 7*3*3*	R L R L	R L R *	R L R *	R L R *
L- 7*3*3*	L R L R	L R L *	L R L *	L R L *

3-5-5

R- 3*5*5*	R L R *	R L R L	R * R L	R L R *
L- 3*5*5*	L R L *	L R L R	L * L R	L R L *
R- 5*3*5*	R L R L	R * R L	R * R L	R L R *
L- 5*3*5*	L R L R	L * L R	L * L R	L R L *
R- 5*5*3*	R L R L	R * R L	R L R *	R L R *
L- 5*5*3*	L R L R	L * L R	L R L *	L R L *

BIMANUAL DEXTERITY

LESSON ONE
BASICS LINE BY LINE RIGHT AND LEFT

3-1-3-1-3

R- 3*1*3*1*3*	R L R *	R * R L	R * R *	R L R *
L- 3*1*3*1*3*	L R L *	L * L R	L * L *	L R L *
R- 1*3*3*1*3*	R * R L	R * R L	R * R *	R L R *
L- 1*3*3*1*3*	L * L R	L * L R	L * L *	L R L *
R- 1*3*1*3*3*	R * R L	R * R *	R L R *	R L R *
L- 1*3*1*3*3*	L * L R	L * L *	L R L *	L R L *
R- 3*3*1*3*1*	R L R *	R L R *	R * R L	R * R *
L- 3*3*1*3*1*	L R L *	L R L *	L * L R	L * L *
R- 3*1*3*3*1*	R L R *	R * R L	R * R L	R * R *
L- 3*1*3*3*1*	L R L *	L * L R	L * L R	L * L *
R- 1*1*3*3*3*	R * R *	R L R *	R L R *	R L R *
L- 1*1*3*3*3*	L * L *	L R L *	L R L *	L R L *
R- 3*1*1*3*3*	R L R *	R * R *	R L R *	R L R *
L- 3*1*1*3*3*	L R L *	L * L *	L R L *	L R L *
R- 3*3*1*1*3*	R L R *	R L R *	R * R *	R L R *
L- 3*3*1*1*3*	L R L *	L R L *	L * L *	L R L *
R- 3*3*3*1*1*	R L R *	R L R *	R L R *	R * R *
L- 3*3*3*1*1*	L R L *	L R L *	L R L *	L * L *

BIMANUAL DEXTERITY

LESSON ONE
BASICS LINE BY LINE RIGHT AND LEFT

5-1-5-1

R- 5*1*5*1*	R L R L	R * R *	R L R L	R * R *
L- 5*1*5*1*	L R L R	L * L *	L R L R	L * L *
R- 5*1*1*5*	R L R L	R * R *	R * R L	R L R *
L- 5*1*1*5*	L R L R	L * L *	L * L R	L R L *
R- 5*5*1*1*	R L R L	R * R L	R L R *	R * R *
L- 5*5*1*1*	L R L R	L * L R	L R L *	L * L *
R- 1*1*5*5*	R * R *	R L R L	R * R L	R L R *
L- 1*1*5*5*	L * L *	L R L R	L * L R	L R L *
R- 1*5*1*5*	R * R L	R L R *	R * R L	R L R *
L- 1*5*1*5*	L * L R	L R L *	L * L R	L R L *
R- 1*5*5*1*	R * R L	R L R *	R L R L	R * R *
L- 1*5*5*1*	L * L R	L R L *	L R L R	L * L *

RHYTHM FACTORING

BIMANUAL DEXTERITY

LESSON ONE
BASICS LINE BY LINE RIGHT AND LEFT

3-5-1-3

R—3*5*1*3*	R L R *	R L R L	R * R *	R L R *
L--3*5*1*3*	L R L *	L R L R	L * L *	L R L *
R—5*1*3*3*	R L R L	R * R *	R L R *	R L R *
L--5*1*3*3*	L R L R	L * L *	L R L *	L R L *
R—1*3*3*5*	R * R L	R * R L	R * R L	R L R *
L--1*3*3*5*	L * L R	L * L R	L * L R	L R L *
R—1*3*5*3*	R * R L	R * R L	R L R *	R L R *
L--1*3*5*3*	L * L R	L * L R	L R L *	L R L *
R—1*5*3*3*	R * R L	R L R *	R L R *	R L R *
L--1*5*3*3*	L * L R	L R L *	L R L *	L R L *
R—5*3*3*1*	R L R L	R * R L	R * R L	R * R *
L--5*3*3*1*	L R L R	L * L R	L * L R	L * L *
R—5*3*1*3*	R L R L	R * R L	R * R *	R L R *
L--5*3*1*3*	L R L R	L * L R	L * L *	L R L *
R—3*1*5*3*	R L R *	R * R L	R L R *	R L R *
L--3*1*5*3*	L R L *	L * L R	L R L *	L R L *
R—3*3*1*5*	R L R *	R L R *	R * R L	R L R *
L--3*3*1*5*	L R L *	L R L *	L * L R	L R L *
R—3*5*3*1*	R L R *	R L R L	R * R L	R * R *
L--3*5*3*1*	L R L *	L R L R	L * L R	L * L *

BIMANUAL DEXTERITY

LESSON ONE
BASICS LINE BY LINE RIGHT AND LEFT

7-1-5

R- 7*1*5*	R L R L	R L R *	R * R L	R L R *
L- 7*1*5*	L R L R	L R L *	L * L R	L R L *
R- 7*5*1*	R L R L	R L R *	R L R L	R * R *
L- 7*5*1*	L R L R	L R L *	L R L R	L * L *
R- 5*7*1*	R L R L	R * R L	R L R L	R * R *
L- 5*7*1*	L R L R	L * L R	L R L R	L * L *
R- 5*1*7*	R L R L	R * R *	R L R L	R L R *
L- 5*1*7*	L R L R	L * L *	L R L R	L R L *
R- 1*7*5*	R * R L	R L R L	R * R L	R L R *
L- 1*7*5*	L * L R	L R L R	L * L R	L R L *
R- 1*5*7*	R * R L	R L R *	R L R L	R L R *
L- 1*5*7*	L * L R	L R L *	L R L R	L R L *

BIMANUAL DEXTERITY

LESSON ONE
BASICS LINE BY LINE RIGHT AND LEFT

3-1-1-5-1

R- 3*1*1*5*1*	R L R *	R * R *	R L R L	R * R *
L- 3*1*1*5*1*	L R L *	L * L *	L R L R	L * L *
R- 3*1*1*1*5	R L R *	R * R *	R * R L	R L R *
L- 3*1*1*1*5	L R L *	L * L *	L * L R	L R L *
R- 3*1*5*1*1*	R L R *	R * R L	R L R *	R * R *
L- 3*1*5*1*1*	L R L *	L * L R	L R L *	L * L *
R- 3*5*1*1*1*	R L R *	R L R L	R * R *	R * R *
L- 3*5*1*1*1*	L R L *	L R L R	L * L *	L * L *
R- 5*3*1*1*1*	R L R L	R * R L	R * R *	R * R *
L- 5*3*1*1*1*	L R L R	L * L R	L * L *	L * L *
R- 5*1*1*1*3*	R L R L	R * R *	R * R *	R L R *
L- 5*1*1*1*3*	L R L R	L * L *	L * L *	L R L *
R- 5*1*1*3*1*	R L R L	R * R *	R * R L	R * R *
L- 5*1*1*3*1*	L R L R	L * L *	L * L R	L * L *
R- 5*1*3*1*1*	R L R L	R * R *	R L R *	R * R *
L- 5*1*3*1*1*	L R L R	L * L *	L R L *	L * L *
R- 1*5*1*1*3*	R * R L	R L R *	R * R *	R L R *
L- 1*5*1*1*3*	L * L R	L R L *	L * L *	L R L *
R- 1*5*1*3*1*	R * R L	R L R *	R * R L	R * R *
L- 1*5*1*3*1*	L * L R	L R L *	L * L R	L * L *

BIMANUAL DEXTERITY

LESSON ONE
BASICS LINE BY LINE RIGHT AND LEFT

3-1-7-1

R- 3*1*7*1*	R L R *	R * R L	R L R L	R * R *
L- 3*1*7*1*	L R L *	L * L R	L R L R	L * L *
R- 3*1*1*7*	R L R *	R * R *	R L R L	R L R *
L- 3*1*1*7*	L R L *	L * L *	L R L R	L R L *
R- 3*7*1*1*	R L R *	R L R L	R L R *	R * R *
L- 3*7*1*1*	L R L *	L R L R	L R L *	L * L *
R- 7*1*1*3*	R L R L	R L R *	R * R *	R L R *
L- 7*1*1*3*	L R L R	L R L *	L * L *	L R L *
R- 7*1*3*1*	R L R L	R L R *	R * R L	R * R *
L- 7*1*3*1*	L R L R	L R L *	L * L R	L * L *
R- 7*3*1*1*	R L R L	R L R *	R L R *	R * R *
L- 7*3*1*1*	L R L R	L R L *	L R L *	L * L *
R- 1*3*7*1*	R * R L	R * R L	R L R L	R * R *
L- 1*3*7*1*	L * L R	L * L R	L R L R	L * L *
R- 1*3*1*7*	R * R L	R * R *	R L R L	R L R *
L- 1*3*1*7*	L * L R	L * L *	L R L R	L R L *
R- 1*7*1*3*	R * R L	R L R L	R * R *	R L R *
L- 1*7*1*3*	L * L R	L R L R	L * L *	L R L *

BIMANUAL DEXTERITY

LESSON ONE
BASICS LINE BY LINE RIGHT AND LEFT

1-3-1-1-1-3

R- 1*3*1*1*1*3*	R * R L	R * R *	R * R *	R L R *
L- 1*3*1*1*1*3	L * L R	L * L *	L * L *	L R L *
R- 1*1*1*3*1*3*	R * R *	R * R L	R * R *	R L R *
L- 1*1*1*3*1*3	L * L *	L * L R	L * L *	L R L *
R- 1*1*1*3*3*1*	R * R *	R * R L	R * R L	R * R *
L- 1*1*1*3*3*1	L * L *	L * L R	L * L R	L * L *
R- 1*1*1*1*3*3*	R * R *	R * R *	R L R *	R L R *
L- 1*1*1*1*3*3	L * L *	L * L *	L R L *	L R L *
R- 1*1*3*3*1*1	R * R *	R L R *	R L R *	R * R *
L- 1*1*3*3*1*1	L * L *	L R L *	L R L *	L * L *
R- 1*1*3*1*3*1	R * R *	R L R *	R * R L	R * R *
L- 1*1*3*1*3*1	L * L *	L R L *	L * L R	L * L *
R- 1*1*3*1*1*3	R * R *	R L R *	R * R *	R L R *
L- 1*1*3*1*1*3	L * L *	L R L *	L * L *	L R L *
R- 1*3*1*1*1*3	R * R L	R * R *	R * R *	R L R *
L- 1*3*1*1*1*3	L * L R	L * L *	L * L *	L R L *
R- 1*3*1*1*3*1	R * R L	R * R *	R * R L	R * R *
L- 1*3*1*1*3*1	L * L R	L * L *	L * L R	L * L *

BIMANUAL DEXTERITY

LESSON TWO
BASICS FACTOR BY FACTOR RIGHT AND LEFT

3-5-5

3*5*5*	R L R *	L R L R	L * R L	R L R *
5*3*5*	L R L R	L * R L	R * L R	L R L *
5*5*3*	R L R L	R * L R	L R L *	R L R *

3-3-7

3*3*7*	R L R *	L R L *	R L R L	R L R *
3*7*3*	L R L *	R L R L	R L R *	L R L *
7*3*3*	R L R L	R L R *	L R L *	R L R *

3-1-3-1-3

3*1*3*1*3*	R L R *	L * R L	R * L *	R L R *
1*3*3*1*3*	L * R L	R * L R	L * R *	L R L *
1*3*1*3*3*	R * L R	L * R *	L R L *	R L R *
3*3*1*3*1*	L R L *	R L R *	L * R L	R * L *
3*1*3*3*1*	R L R *	L * R L	R * L R	L * R *
1*1*3*3*3*	L * R *	L R L *	R L R *	L R L *
3*1*1*3*3*	R L R *	L * R *	L R L *	R L R *
3*3*1*1*3*	L R L *	R L R *	L * R *	L R L *
3*3*3*1*1*	R L R *	L R L *	R L R *	L * R *

BIMANUAL DEXTERITY

LESSON TWO
BASICS FACTOR BY FACTOR RIGHT AND LEFT

5-1-5-1

5*1*5*1*	R L R L	R * L *	R L R L	R * L *
5*1*1*5*	L R L R	L * R *	L * R L	R L R *
5*5*1*1*	R L R L	R * L R	L R L *	R * L *
1*1*5*5*	L * R *	L R L R	L * R L	R L R *
1*5*1*5*	R * L R	L R L *	R * L R	L R L *
1*5*5*1*	L * R L	R L R *	L R L R	L * R *

3-5-1-3

3*5*1*3*	R L R *	L R L R	L * R *	L R L *
5*1*3*3*	L R L R	L * R *	L R L *	R L R *
1*3*3*5*	R * L R	L * R L	R * L R	L R L *
1*3*5*3*	L * R L	R * L R	L R L *	R L R *
1*5*3*3*	R * L R	L R L *	R L R *	L R L *
5*3*3*1*	L R L R	L * R L	R * L R	L * R *
5*3*1*3*	R L R L	R * L R	L * R *	L R L *
3*1*5*3*	L R L *	R * L R	L R L *	R L R *
3*3*1*5*	R L R *	L R L *	R * L R	L R L *
3*5*3*1*	L R L *	R L R L	R * L R	L * R *
3*3*5*1*	R L R *	L R L *	R L R L	R * L *
3*1*3*5*	L R L *	R * L R	L * R L	R L R *

BIMANUAL DEXTERITY

LESSON TWO
BASICS FACTOR BY FACTOR RIGHT AND LEFT

7-1-5

7*1*5*	R L R L	R L R *	L * R L	R L R *
7*5*1*	L R L R	L R L *	R L R L	R * L *
5*7*1*	R L R L	R * L R	L R L R	R * R *
5*1*7*	L R L R	L * R *	L R L R	L R L *
1*7*5*	R * L R	L R L R	L * R L	R L R *
1*5*7*	L * R L	R L R *	L R L R	L R L *

3-1-7-1

3*1*7*1*	R L R *	L * R L	R L R L	R * L *
3*1*1*7*	L R L *	R * L *	R L R L	R L R *
3*7*1*1*	R L R *	L R L R	L R L *	R * L *
7*1*1*3*	L R L R	L R L *	R * L *	R L R *
7*1*3*1*	R L R L	R L R *	L * R L	R * L *
7*3*1*1*	L R L R	L R L *	R L R *	L * R *
1*3*7*1*	R * L R	L * R *	L R L R	L R L *
1*3*1*7*	L * R L	R * L *	R L R L	R L R *
1*7*1*3*	R * L R	L R L R	L * R *	L R L *

BIMANUAL DEXTERITY

LESSON TWO
BASICS FACTOR BY FACTOR RIGHT AND LEFT

3-1-1-5-1

3*1*1*5*1*	R L R *	L * R *	L R L R	L * R *
3*1*1*1*5*	L R L *	R * L *	R * L R	L R L *
3*1*5*1*1*	R L R *	L * R L	R L R *	L * R *
3*5*1*1*1*	L R L *	R L R L	R * L *	R * L *
5*3*1*1*1*	R L R L	R * L R	L * R *	L * R *
5*1*1*1*3*	L R L R	L * R *	L * R *	L R L *
5*1*1*3*1*	R L R L	R * L *	R * L R	L * R *
5*1*3*1*1*	L R L R	L * R *	L R L *	R * L *
1*5*1*1*3*	R * L R	L R L *	R * L *	R L R *
1*5*1*3*1*	L * R L	R L R *	L * R L	R * L *
1*5*3*1*1*	R * L R	L R L *	R L R *	L * R *
1*3*5*1*1*	L * R L	R * L R	L R L *	R * L *
1*3*1*1*5*	R * L R	L * R *	L * R L	R L R *
1*3*1*5*1*	L * R L	R * L *	R L R L	R * L *
1*1*5*3*1*	R * L *	R L R L	R * L R	L * R *
1*1*5*1*3*	L * R *	L R L R	L * R *	L R L *
1*1*3*5*1*	R * L *	R L R *	L R L R	L * R *
1*1*3*1*5*	L * R *	L R L *	R * L R	L R L *
1*1*1*3*5*	R * L *	R * L R	L * R L	R L R *

RHYTHM FACTORING

BIMANUAL DEXTERITY

LESSON TWO
BASICS FACTOR BY FACTOR RIGHT AND LEFT

1-3-1-1-1-3

1*3*1*1*1*3	R * L R	L * R *	L * R *	L R L *
1*1*1*3*1*3	L * R *	L * L R	L * R *	L R L*
1*1*1*3*3*1	R * L *	R * L R	L * R L	R * L *
1*1*1*1*3*3	L * R *	L * R *	L R L *	R L R *
1*1*1*3*1*3	R * L *	R * L R	L * R *	L R L *
1*1*3*3*1*1	L * R *	L R L *	R L R *	L * R *
1*1*3*1*3*1	R * L *	R L R *	L * R L	R * L *
1*1*3*1*1*3	L * R *	L R L *	R * L *	R L R *
1*3*1*1*1*3	R * L R	L * R *	L * R *	L R L *
1*3*1*1*3*1	L * R L	R * L *	R * L R	L * R *
1*3*3*1*1*1	R * L R	L * R L	R * L *	R * L *
3*1*1*1*1*3	L R L *	R * L *	R * L *	R L R *
3*1*1*1*3*1	R L R *	L * R *	L * R L	R * L *
3*1*1*3*1*1	L R L *	R * L *	R L R *	L * R *
3*1*3*1*1*1	R L R *	L * R L	R * L *	R * L *

SECTION 7

RHYTHM SONG LIBRARY

RHYTHM SONG LIBRARY

INTRODUCTION TO RHYTHM SONG LIBRARY

The songs in this library are simple constructions, offered to reiterate the concepts of factoring offered in this book. The songs correspond with the Lesson-by-Lesson format of the course from start to finish, integrating deeper learning and increased musicality. The song library can be played song by song after completing the entire course, as a review and integration exercise or the songs can be learned and played along with the related lessons.

SONG BUILDING

Songs can vary in shape and complexity, some with only one phrase repeated continuously, others with many distinct parts joined together in intricate ways. Songs are made of musical phrases strung together artfully. Choruses Tend to be more repetitive, while verses are more lyrical.

PHRASING

Phrases are pieces of a song strung together in a particular order- a pattern arrangement which can communicate mood, story, and emotion; music is built on numbers. Musical phrases can be either lyrical or repetitive in nature.

SONG SHAPING

The songs in this library all follow a simple recipe, laid out with a fixed number of verses and choruses- simple songs containing two verses, with 3 pattern combination, and two choruses, with 2 pattern combinations. The only variation in form comes from the addition of three songs with bridges This simplicity enables deeper learning of the complex factor patterning method described throughout this book.

SONG SHAPING VARIATIONS

It is possible to shape songs in many ways. Creativity in the shaping of songs is a great marker of musical richness. While the songs in this collection are very simple in nature, this rhythm method can be adapted to fit with complex song building strategies.

RHYTHM SONG LIBRARY

SONGS FOR SECTION ONE- BASIC PATTERNS

BASIC PATTERNS Simple factors
1) RIGHT Basic 3's and 3*3*7* and 7*7* and 3*5*5* and 5*3*5*
2) LEFT Basic 3's and 3*3*7* and 7*7* and 3*5*5* and 5*3*5*
3) RIGHT Basic 3's and 3*1*3*1*3* and 3*3*7* and 3*1*1*1*1*3* and 1*3*1*1*1*3*
4) LEFT Basic 3's and 3*1*3*1*3* and 3*3*7* and 3*1*1*1*1*3* and 1*3*1*1*1*3*

BASIC PATTERNS Combined factors
5) RIGHT 3*5*1*3* and 5*1*1*1*3* and 5*5*3* and 5*1*5*1* and 5*1*7*
6) LEFT 3*5*1*3* and 5*1*1*1*3* and 5*5*3* and 5*1*5*1* and 5*1*7*
7) RIGHT 3*1*3*3*1* and 3*1*7*1* and 7*5*1* and 7*1*5* and 5*1*7*
8) LEFT 3*1*3*3*1* and 3*1*7*1* and 7*5*1* and 7*1*5* and 5*1*7*
9) RIGHT 3*1*1*7* and 5*1*7* and 5*1*1*1*3* and 3*1*1*1*3*1* and 3*1*1*3*1*1*…
10) LEFT 3*1*1*7* and 5*1*7* and 5*1*1*1*3* and 3*1*1*1*3*1* and 3*1*1*3*1*1*…

SONGS FOR SECTION TWO- ACCENT VARIATIONS

11) STANDARD Basic 3's and 7*7* and 5*5*3* and 3*7*3* and 1*1*3*3*3* and 1*3*1*1*1*3*
12) CENTER Basic 3's and 7*7* and 5*5*3* and 3*7*3* and 1*1*3*3*3* and 1*3*1*1*1*3*
13) REVERSE Basic 3's and 7*7* and 5*5*3* and 3*7*3* and 1*1*3*3*3* and 1*3*1*1*1*3*
14) STANDARD 1*5*1*5* and 5*3*1*3* and 7*1*1*3* and 1*7*5* and 5*3*1*1*1*
15) CENTER 1*5*1*5* and 5*3*1*3* and 7*1*1*3* and 1*7*5* and 5*3*1*1*1*
16) REVERSE 1*5*1*5* and 5*3*1*3* and 7*1*1*3* and 1*7*5* and 5*3*1*1*1*

SONGS FOR SECTION THREE- DRUM NOTATION

17)- DRUM- Basic 3'S and 3*3*7* and 7*7* and 3*5*5* and 5*3*5*
18)- DRUM- Basic 3'S and 3*1*3*1*3* and 3*3*7* and 3*1*1*1*1*3* and 1*3*1*1*1*3*
19)- DRUM-3*5*1*3* and 5*1*1*1*3* and 5*5*3* and 5*1*5*1* and 5*1*7*

RHYTHM SONG LIBRARY

SONGS FOR SECTION FOUR- SYNCOPATION

SYNCOPATED 4's
20) SYNC FOUR Basic 3's and 3*4*4* and 5*4*3* and 7*1*4* and 3*1*3*4*
21) SYNC FOUR 5*1*4*1* and 3*4*3*1* and 4*4*1*1* and 3*1*4*1*1*

SYNCOPATED 2's
22) SYNC TWO- Basic 2's and 2*5*5* and 2*3*1*5* and 3*2*2*3* and 3*2*7*
23) SYNC TWO 2*7*1*1* and 2*7*2* and 3*2*3*1*1* and 2*5*1*2* and 2*1*1*2*2*

SYNCOPATED 2's and 4's
24) SYNC TWO-FOUR- 2*4*5* and 4*1*2*3* and 2*5*5* and 2*2*7* and 2*3*7*
25) SYNC TWO-FOUR - 4*4*1*1* and 4*4*3* and 4*4*2* and 4*1*2*3* and 7*1*1*2* and 7*1*4*

SONGS FOR SECTION FIVE- 6 BEAT TIMING VARIATION

26) Basic 3's and 3*7*3*7* and 3*7*5*1*3* and 3*3*3*7*3* and 7*7*7*
27) 3*5*1*3*5*1* and 7*3*7*3* and 5*3*1*5*3*1* and 3*1*3*1*3*1*3*1* and 3*3*1*1*7*1*1*
28) 1*5*1*1*1*5*1*1* and 7*1*1*7*1*1* and 1*3*1*3*1*7*1* and 3*3*3*1*1*3*3* and 3*7*5*1*3*

SONGS FOR SECTION SIX- BIMANUAL DEXTERITY

RIGHT AND LEFT by factor
29) Basic 3's and 3*3*7* and 7*7* and 3*5*5* and 5*3*5*
30) Basic 3's and 3*1*3*1*3* and 3*3*7* and 3*1*1*1*1*3* and 1*3*1*1*1*3*

SONG FOR SECTION NINE- FINGER CYMBAL DANCE
31)- EMBODIED RHYTHM MOVEMENT PRACTICE- Thirteen figure group circle dance

RHYTHM SONG LIBRARY

SECTION 1- SONG 1
BASIC PATTERNS- right hand
Basic 3'S and 3*3*7* and 7*7* and 3*5*5* and 5*3*5*

VERSE

A) Basic 3's	R L R *	R L R *	R L R *	R L R *
B) 3*3*7*	R L R *	R L R *	R L R L	R L R *
B) 3*3*7*	R L R *	R L R *	R L R L	R L R *
C) 7*7*	R L R L	R L R *	R L R L	R L R *

CHORUS

D) 3*5*5*	R L R *	R L R L	R * R L	R L R *
D) 3*5*5*	R L R *	R L R L	R * R L	R L R *
D) 3*5*5*	R L R *	R L R L	R * R L	R L R *
E) 5*3*5*	R L R L	R * R L	R * R L	R L R *

VERSE REPEAT

ENDING CHORUS

D) 3*5*5*	R L R *	R L R L	R * R L	R L R *
D) 3*5*5*	R L R *	R L R L	R * R L	R L R *
D) 3*5*5*	R L R *	R L R L	R * R L	R L R *
E) 5*3*5*	R L R L	R * R L	R * R L	R L R *
Z) Singles*	R L R L	R L R L	R L R L	R L R L
Z) Singles*	R L R L	R L R L	R L R L	R L R *

RHYTHM FACTORING

RHYTHM SONG LIBRARY

SECTION 1- SONG 2
BASIC PATTERNS- left hand
Basic 3'S and 3*3*7* and 7*7* and 3*5*5* and 5*3*5*

VERSE

A) Basic 3's	L R L *	L R L *	L R L *	L R L *
B) 3*3*7*	L R L *	L R L *	L R L R	L R L *
B) 3*3*7*	L R L *	L R L *	L R L R	L R L *
C) 7*7*	L R L L	L R L *	L R L R	L R L *

CHORUS

D) 3*5*5*	L R L *	L R L R	L * L R	L R L *
D) 3*5*5*	L R L *	L R L R	L * L R	L R L *
D) 3*5*5*	L R L *	L R L R	L * L R	L R L *
E) 5*3*5*	L R L R	L * L R	L * L R	L R L *

VERSE REPEAT

ENDING CHORUS

D) 3*5*5*	L R L *	L R L R	L * L R	L R L *
D) 3*5*5*	L R L *	L R L R	L * L R	L R L *
D) 3*5*5*	L R L *	L R L R	L * L R	L R L *
E) 5*3*5*	L R L R	L * L R	L * L R	L R L *
Z) Singles*	L R L R	L R L R	L R L R	L R L R
Z) Singles*	L R L R	L R L R	L R L R	L R L *

RHYTHM FACTORING

RHYTHM SONG LIBRARY

SECTION 1- SONG 3
BASIC PATTERNS- right hand
Basic 3'S and 3*1*3*1*3* and 3*3*7* and 3*1*1*1*1*3* and 1*3*1*1*1*3*

VERSE

A) Basic 3's	R L R *	R L R *	R L R *	R L R *
B) 3*1*3*1*3*	R L R *	R * R L	R * R *	R L R *
B) 3*1*3*1*3*	R L R *	R * R L	R ≈ R *	R L R *
C) 3*3*7*	R L R *	R L R *	R L R L	R L R *

CHORUS

D) 3*1*1*1*1*3*	R L R *	R * R *	R * R *	R L R *
E) 1*3*1*1*1*3*	R * R L	R * R *	R * R *	R L R *
E) 1*3*1*1*1*3*	R * R L	R * R *	R * R *	R L R *
D) 3*1*1*1*1*3*	R L R *	R * R *	R * R *	R L R *

VERSE REPEAT

ENDING CHORUS

D) 3*1*1*1*1*3*	R L R *	R * R *	R * R *	R L R *
E) 1*3*1*1*1*3*	R * R L	R * R *	R * R *	R L R *
E) 1*3*1*1*1*3*	R * R L	R * R *	R * R *	R L R *
D) 3*1*1*1*1*3*	R L R *	R * R *	R * R *	R L R *
Z) Singles*	R L R L	R L R L	R L R L	R L R L
Z) Singles*	R L R L	R L R L	R L R L	R L R *

RHYTHM SONG LIBRARY

SECTION 1- SONG 4
BASIC PATTERNS left hand
Basic 3'S and 3*1*3*1*3* and 3*3*7* and 3*1*1*1*1*3* and 1*3*1*1*1*3*

VERSE

A) Basic 3's	L R L *	L R L *	L R L *	L R L *
B) 3*1*3*1*3*	L R L *	L * L R	L * R *	L R L *
B) 3*1*3*1*3*	L R L *	L * L R	L * R *	L R L *
C) 3*3*7*	L R L *	L R L *	L R L R	L R L *

CHORUS

D) 3*1*1*1*1*3*	L R L*	L * L *	L * L *	L R L *
E) 1*3*1*1*3*1*	L * L R	L * L *	L * L R	L * L *
E) 1*3*1*1*1*3*	L * L R	L * L *	L * L *	L R L *
D) 3*1*1*1*1*3*	L R L*	L * L *	L * L *	L R L *

VERSE REPEAT

ENDING CHORUS

D) 3*1*1*1*1*3*	L R L*	L * L *	L * L *	L R L *
E) 1*3*1*1*3*1*	L * L R	L * L *	L * L R	L * L *
E) 1*3*1*1*1*3*	L * L R	L * L *	L * L *	L R L *
D) 3*1*1*1*1*3*	L R L*	L * L *	L * L *	L R L *
Z) Singles*	L R L R	L R L R	L R L R	L R L R
Z) Singles*	L R L R	L R L R	L R L R	L R L *

RHYTHM SONG LIBRARY

SECTION 1- SONG 5
COMBINED PATTERNS- right hand
3*5*1*3* and 5*1*1*1*3* and 5*5*3* and 5*1*5*1* and 5*1*7*

VERSE

A) 3*5*1*3*	R L R *	R L R L	R * R *	R L R *
B) 5*1*1*1*3*	R L R L	R * R *	R * R *	R L R *
C) 5*5*3*	R L R L	R * R L	R L R *	R L R *
B) 5*1*1*1*3*	R L R L	R * R *	R * R *	R L R *

CHORUS

D) 5*1*5*1*	R L R L	R * R *	R L R L	R * R *
E) 5*1*7*	R L R L	R * R *	R L R L	R L R *
D) 5*1*5*1*	R L R L	R * R *	R L R L	R * R *
E) 5*1*7*	R L R L	R * R *	R L R L	R L R *

VERSE REPEAT

ENDING CHORUS

D) 5*1*5*1*	R L R L	R * R *	R L R L	R * R *
E) 5*1*7*	R L R L	R * R *	R L R L	R L R *
D) 5*1*5*1*	R L R L	R * R *	R L R L	R * R *
E) 5*1*7*	R L R L	R * R *	R L R L	R L R *
Z) Singles*	R L R L	R L R L	R L R L	R L R L
Z) Singles*	L R L R	L R L R	L R L R	L R L *

RHYTHM FACTORING

RHYTHM SONG LIBRARY

SECTION 1- SONG 6
COMBINED PATTERNS- left hand
3*5*1*3* and 5*1*1*1*3* and 5*5*3* and 5*1*5*1* and 5*1*7*

VERSE

A) 3*5*1*3*	L R L *	L R L R	L * L *	L R L *
B) 5*1*1*1*3*	L R L R	L * L *	L * L *	L R L *
C) 5*5*3	L R L R	L * L R	L R L *	L R L *
B) 5*1*1*1*3*	L R L R	L * L *	L * L *	L R L *

CHORUS

D) 5*1*5*1*	L R L R	L * L *	L R L R	L * L *
E) 5*1*7*	L R L R	L * L *	L R L R	L R L *
D) 5*1*5*1*	L R L R	L * L *	L R L R	L * L *
E) 5*1*7*	L R L R	L * L *	L R L R	L R L *

VERSE REPEAT

ENDING CHORUS

D) 5*1*5*1*	L R L R	L * L *	L R L R	L * L *
E) 5*1*7*	L R L R	L * L *	L R L R	L R L *
D) 5*1*5*1*	L R L R	L * L *	L R L R	L * L *
E) 5*1*7*	L R L R	L * L *	L R L R	L R L *
Z) Singles*	L R L R	L R L R	L R L R	L R L R
Z) Singles*	L R L R	L R L R	L R L R	L R L *

RHYTHM FACTORING

RHYTHM SONG LIBRARY

SECTION 1- SONG 7
COMBINED PATTERNS right hand
3*1*3*3*1* and 3*1*7*1* and 7*5*1* and 7*1*5* and 5*1*7*

VERSE

A) 3*1*3*3*1*	R L R *	R * R L	R * R L	R * R *
B) 3*1*7*1*	R L R *	R * R L	R L R L	R * R *
B) 3*1*7*1*	R L R *	R * R L	R L R L	R * R *
C) 7*1*5*	R L R L	R L R *	R * R L	R L R *

CHORUS

D) 7*1*5*	R L R L	R L R *	R * R L	R L R *
E) 5*1*7*	R L R L	R * R *	R L R L	R L R *
D) 7*1*5*	R L R L	R L R *	R * R L	R L R *
E) 5*1*7*	R L R L	R * R *	R L R L	R L R *

VERSE REPEAT

ENDING CHORUS

D) 7*1*5*	R L R L	R L R *	R * R L	R L R *
E) 5*1*7*	R L R L	R * R *	R L R L	R L R *
D) 7*1*5*	R L R L	R L R *	R * R L	R L R *
E) 5*1*7*	R L R L	R * R *	R L R L	R L R *
Z) Singles*	R L R L	R L R L	R L R L	R L R L
Z) Singles*	R L R L	R L R L	R L R L	R L R *

RHYTHM FACTORING

RHYTHM SONG LIBRARY

SECTION 1- SONG 8
COMBINED PATTERNS- left hand
3*1*3*3*1* and 3*1*7*1* and 7*5*1* and 7*1*5* and 5*1*7*

VERSE

A) 3*1*3*3*1*	L R L *	L * L R	L * L R	L * L *
B) 3*1*7*1*	L R L *	L * L R	L R L R	L * L *
B) 3*1*7*1*	L R L *	L * L R	L R L R	L * L *
C) 7*1*5*	L R L R	L R L *	L * L R	L R L *

CHORUS

D) 7*1*5*	L R L R	L R L *	L * L R	L R L *
E) 5*1*7*	L R L R	L * L *	L R L R	L R L *
D) 7*1*5*	L R L R	L R L *	L * L R	L R L *
E) 5*1*7*	L R L R	L * L *	L R L R	L R L *

VERSE REPEAT

ENDING CHORUS

D) 7*1*5*	L R L R	L R L *	L * L R	L R L *
E) 5*1*7*	L R L R	L * L *	L R L R	L R L *
D) 7*1*5*	L R L R	L R L *	L * L R	L R L *
E) 5*1*7*	L R L R	L * L *	L R L R	L R L *
Z) Singles*	L R L R	L R L R	L R L R	L R L R
Z) Singles*	L R L R	L R L R	L R L R	L R L *

RHYTHM SONG LIBRARY

SECTION 1- SONG 9
COMBINED PATTERNS right hand
3*1*1*7* - 5*1*7* - 5*1*1*1*3* - 3*1*1*1**3*1* - 3*1*1*3*1*1* - 3*1*3*1*1*1* - 5*7*1*

VERSE

A) 3*1*1*7*	R L R *	R * R *	R L R L	R L R *
B) 5*1*7*	R L R L	R * R *	R L R L	R L R *
B) 5*1*7*	R L R L	R * R *	R L R L	R L R *
C) 5*1*1*1*3*	R L R L	R * R *	R * R *	R L R *

CHORUS

D) 3*1*1*1*3*1*	R L R *	R * R *	R * R L	R * R *
E) 3*1*1*3*1*1*	R L R *	R * R *	R L R *	R * R *
F) 3*1*3*1*1*1*	R L R *	R * R L	R * R *	R * R *
G) 5*7*1*	R L R L	R * R L	R L R L	R * R *

VERSE REPEAT

ENDING CHORUS

D) 3*1*1*1*3*1*	R L R *	R * R *	R * R L	R * R *
E) 3*1*1*3*1*1*	R L R *	R * R *	R L R *	R * R *
F) 3*1*3*1*1*1*	R L R *	R * R L	R * R *	R * R *
G) 5*7*1*	R L R L	R * R L	R L R L	R * R *
Z) Singles*	R L R L	R L R L	R L R L	R L R *
Z) Singles*	R L R L	R L R L	R L R L	R L R *

RHYTHM SONG LIBRARY

SECTION 1- SONG 10
COMBINED PATTERNS-left hand
3*1*1*7* - 5*1*7* - 5*1*1*1*3* - 3*1*1*1**3*1* - 3*1*1*3*1*1* - 3*1*3*1*1*1* - 5*7*1*

VERSE

A) 3*1*1*7*	L R L *	L * L *	L R L R	L R L *
B) 5*1*7*	L R L R	L * L *	L R L R	L R L *
B) 5*1*7*	L R L R	L * L *	L R L R	L R L *
C) 5*1*1*1*3*	L R L R	L * L *	L * L *	L R L *

CHORUS

D) 3*1*1*1*3*1*	L R L *	L * L *	L * L R	L * L *
E) 3*1*1*3*1*1*	L R L *	L * L *	L R L *	L * L *
F) 3*1*3*1*1*1*	L R L *	L * L R	L * L *	L * L *
G) 5*7*1*	L R L R	L * L R	L R L R	L * L *

VERSE REPEAT

ENDING CHORUS

D) 3*1*1*1*3*1*	L R L *	L * L *	L * L R	L * L *
E) 3*1*1*3*1*1*	L R L *	L * L *	L R L *	L * L *
F) 3*1*3*1*1*1*	L R L *	L * L R	L * L *	L * L *
G) 5*7*1*	L R L R	L * L R	L R L R	L * L *
Z) Singles*	L R L R	L R L R	L R L R	L R L R
Z) Singles*	L R L R	L R L R	L R L R	L R L *

RHYTHM SONG LIBRARY

SECTION 2- SONG 11
ACCENT VARIATIONS- standard
Basic 3'S and 3*3*7* and 7*7* and 3*5*5* and 5*3*5*

VERSE

A) Basic 3's	R L <u>R</u> *	R L <u>R</u> *	R L <u>R</u> *	R L <u>R</u> *
B) 3*3*7*	R L <u>R</u> *	R L <u>R</u> *	R L R L	R L <u>R</u> *
B) 3*3*7*	R L <u>R</u> *	R L <u>R</u> *	R L R L	R L <u>R</u> *
C) 7*7*	R L R L	R L <u>R</u> *	R L R L	R L <u>R</u> *

CHORUS

D) 3*5*5*	R L <u>R</u> *	R L R L	<u>R</u> * R L	R L <u>R</u> *
D) 3*5*5*	R L <u>R</u> *	R L R L	<u>R</u> * R L	R L <u>R</u> *
D) 3*5*5*	R L <u>R</u> *	R L R L	<u>R</u> * R L	R L <u>R</u> *
E) 5*3*5*	R L R L	<u>R</u> * R L	<u>R</u> * R L	R L <u>R</u> *

VERSE REPEAT

ENDING CHORUS

D) 3*5*5*	R L <u>R</u> *	R L R L	<u>R</u> * R L	R L <u>R</u> *
D) 3*5*5*	R L <u>R</u> *	R L R L	<u>R</u> * R L	R L <u>R</u> *
D) 3*5*5*	R L <u>R</u> *	R L R L	<u>R</u> * R L	R L <u>R</u> *
E) 5*3*5*	R L R L	<u>R</u> * R L	<u>R</u> * R L	R L <u>R</u> *
Z) Singles*	R L R L	R L R L	R L R L	R L R L
Z) Singles*	R L R L	R L R L	R L R L	R L <u>R</u> *

RHYTHM FACTORING

RHYTHM SONG LIBRARY

SECTION 2- SONG 12
ACCENT VARIATIONS- center
Basic 3'S and 3*3*7* and 7*7* and 3*5*5* and 5*3*5*

VERSE

A) Basic 3's	R **L** R *	R **L** R *	R **L** R *	R **L** R *
B) 3*3*7*	R **L** R *	R **L** R *	R L R **L**	R L R *
B) 3*3*7*	R **L** R *	R **L** R *	R L R **L**	R L R *
C) 7*7*	R L R **L**	R L R *	R L R **L**	R L R *

CHORUS

D) 3*5*5*	R **L** R *	R L **R** L	R * R L	**R** L R *
D) 3*5*5*	R **L** R *	R L **R** L	R * R L	**R** L R *
D) 3*5*5*	R **L** R *	R L **R** L	R * R L	**R** L R *
E) 5*3*5*	R L **R** L	R * R **L**	R * R L	**R** L R *

VERSE REPEAT

ENDING CHORUS

D) 3*5*5*	R **L** R *	R L R L	R * R L	**R** L R *
D) 3*5*5*	R **L** R *	R L **R** L	R * R L	**R** L R *
D) 3*5*5*	R **L** R *	R L **R** L	R * R L	**R** L R *
E) 5*3*5*	R L **R** L	R * R **L**	R * R L	**R** L R *
Z) Singles*	R L R L	R L R L	R L R L	R L R L
Z) Singles*	R L R L	R L R L	R L R L	R L **R** *

RHYTHM FACTORING

RHYTHM SONG LIBRARY

SECTION 2- SONG 13
ACCENT VARIATIONS reverse
Basic 3'S and 3*3*7* and 7*7* and 3*5*5* and 5*3*5*

VERSE

A) Basic 3's	<u>R</u> L R *	<u>R</u> L R *	<u>R</u> L R *	<u>R</u> L R *
B) 3*3*7*	<u>R</u> L R *	<u>R</u> L R *	<u>R</u> L R L	R L R *
B) 3*3*7*	<u>R</u> L R *	<u>R</u> L R *	<u>R</u> L R L	R L R *
C) 7*7*	<u>R</u> L R L	R L R *	<u>R</u> L R L	R L R *

CHORUS

D) 3*5*5*	<u>R</u> L R *	<u>R</u> L R L	R * <u>R</u> L	R L R *
D) 3*5*5*	<u>R</u> L R *	<u>R</u> L R L	R * <u>R</u> L	R L R *
D) 3*5*5*	<u>R</u> L R *	<u>R</u> L R L	R * <u>R</u> L	R L R *
E) 5*3*5*	<u>R</u> L R L	R * <u>R</u> L	R * <u>R</u> L	R L R *

VERSE REPEAT

ENDING CHORUS

D) 3*5*5*	<u>R</u> L R *	<u>R</u> L R L	R * <u>R</u> L	R L R *
D) 3*5*5*	<u>R</u> L R *	<u>R</u> L R L	R * <u>R</u> L	R L R *
D) 3*5*5*	<u>R</u> L R *	<u>R</u> L R L	R * <u>R</u> L	R L R *
E) 5*3*5*	<u>R</u> L R L	R * <u>R</u> L	R * <u>R</u> L	R L R *
Z) Singles*	R L R L	R L R L	R L R L	R L R L
Z) Singles*	R L R L	R L R L	R L R L	R L <u>R</u> *

RHYTHM SONG LIBRARY

SECTION 2- SONG 14
ACCENT VARIATIONS standard
1*5*1*5* and 5*3*1*3* and 7*1*1*3* and 1*7*5* and 5*3*1*1*

VERSE

A) 1*5*1*5*	<u>R</u> * R L	R L <u>R</u> *	<u>R</u> * R L	R L <u>R</u> *
B) 5*3*1*3*	R L R L	<u>R</u> * R L	<u>R</u> * <u>R</u> *	R L <u>R</u> *
A) 1*5*1*5*	<u>R</u> * R L	R L <u>R</u> *	<u>R</u> * R L	R L <u>R</u> *
C) 7*1*1*3*	R L R L	R L <u>R</u> *	<u>R</u> * <u>R</u> *	R L <u>R</u> *

CHORUS

D) 1*7*5*	<u>R</u> * R L	R L R L	<u>R</u> * R L	R L <u>R</u> *
D) 1*7*5*	<u>R</u> * R L	R L R L	<u>R</u> * R L	R L <u>R</u> *
D) 1*7*5*	<u>R</u> * R L	R L R L	<u>R</u> * R L	R L <u>R</u> *
E) 5*3*1*1*1*	R L R L	<u>R</u> * R L	<u>R</u> * <u>R</u> *	<u>R</u> * <u>R</u> *

VERSE REPEAT

ENDING CHORUS

D) 1*7*5*	<u>R</u> * R L	R L R L	<u>R</u> * R L	R L <u>R</u> *
D) 1*7*5*	<u>R</u> * R L	R L R L	<u>R</u> * R L	R L <u>R</u> *
D) 1*7*5*	<u>R</u> * R L	R L R L	<u>R</u> * R L	R L <u>R</u> *
E) 5*3*1*1*1*	R L R L	<u>R</u> * R L	<u>R</u> * <u>R</u> *	<u>R</u> * <u>R</u> *
Z) Singles*	R L R L	R L R L	R L R L	R L R L
Z) Singles*	R L R L	R L R L	R L R L	R L <u>R</u> *

RHYTHM FACTORING

RHYTHM SONG LIBRARY

SECTION 2- SONG 15
ACCENT VARIATIONS- center
1*5*1*5* and 5*3*1*3* and 7*1*1*3* and 1*7*5* and 5*3*1*1*

VERSE

A) 1*5*1*5*	<u>R</u> * R L	<u>R</u> L R *	<u>R</u> * R L	<u>R</u> L R *
B) 5*3*1*3*	R L <u>R</u> L	R * R <u>L</u>	R * <u>R</u> *	R <u>L</u> R *
A) 1*5*1*5*	<u>R</u> * R L	<u>R</u> L R *	<u>R</u> * R L	<u>R</u> L R *
C) 7*1*1*3*	R L R <u>L</u>	R L R *	<u>R</u> * <u>R</u> *	R <u>L</u> R *

CHORUS

D) 1*7*5*	<u>R</u> * R L	R <u>L</u> R L	R * R L	<u>R</u> L R *
D) 1*7*5*	<u>R</u> * R L	R <u>L</u> R L	R * R L	<u>R</u> L R *
D) 1*7*5*	<u>R</u> * R L	R <u>L</u> R L	R * R L	<u>R</u> L R *
E) 5*3*1*1*1*	R L <u>R</u> L	R * R <u>L</u>	R * <u>R</u> *	R * <u>R</u> *

VERSE REPEAT

ENDING CHORUS

D) 1*7*5*	<u>R</u> * R L	R L R L	R * R L	<u>R</u> L R *
D) 1*7*5*	<u>R</u> * R L	R <u>L</u> R L	R * R L	<u>R</u> L R *
D) 1*7*5*	<u>R</u> * R L	R <u>L</u> R L	R * R L	<u>R</u> L R *
E) 5*3*1*1*1*	R L <u>R</u> L	R * R <u>L</u>	R * <u>R</u> *	<u>R</u> * <u>R</u> *
Z) Singles*	R L R L	R L R L	R L R L	R L R L
Z) Singles*	R L R L	R L R L	R L R L	R L <u>R</u> *

RHYTHM SONG LIBRARY

SECTION 2- SONG 16
ACCENT VARIATIONS- reverse
1*5*1*5* and 5*3*1*3* and 7*1*1*3* and 1*7*5* and 5*3*1*1*

VERSE

A) 1*5*1*5*	R * R L	R L R *	R * R L	R L R *
B) 5*3*1*3*	R L R L	R * R L	R * R *	R L R *
A) 1*5*1*5*	R * R L	R L R *	R * R L	R L R *
C) 7*1*1*3*	R L R L	R L R *	R * R *	R L R *

CHORUS

D) 1*7*5*	R * R L	R L R L	R * R L	R L R *
D) 1*7*5*	R * R L	R L R L	R * R L	R L R *
D) 1*7*5*	R * R L	R L R L	R * R L	R L R *
E) 5*3*1*1*1*	R L R L	R * R L	R * R *	R * R *

VERSE REPEAT

ENDING CHORUS

D) 1*7*5*	R * R L	R L R L	R * R L	R L R *
D) 1*7*5*	R * R L	R L R L	R * R L	R L R *
D) 1*7*5*	R * R L	R L R L	R * R L	R L R *
E) 5*3*1*1*1*	R L R L	R * R L	R * R *	R * R *
Z) Singles*	R L R L	R L R L	R L R L	R L R L
Z) Singles*	R L R L	R L R L	R L R L	R L R *

RHYTHM SONG LIBRARY

SECTION 3- SONG 17
DRUM NOTATION
Basic 3'S and 3*3*7* and 7*7* and 3*5*5* and 5*3*5*

VERSE

A) Basic 3's	Tek Ka Doom *	Tek Ka Doom *	Tek Ka Doom *	Tek Ka Doom *
B) 3*3*7*	Tek Ka Doom *	Tek Ka Doom *	Tek Ka Tek Ka	Tek Ka Doom *
B) 3*3*7*	Tek Ka Doom *	Tek Ka Doom *	Tek Ka Tek Ka	Tek Ka Doom *
C) 7*7*	Tek Ka Tek Ka	Tek Ka Doom *	Tek Ka Tek Ka	Tek Ka Doom *

CHORUS

D) 3*5*5*	Tek Ka Doom *	Tek Ka Tek Ka	Doom * Tek Ka	Tek Ka Doom *
D) 3*5*5*	Tek Ka Doom *	Tek Ka Tek Ka	Doom * Tek Ka	Tek Ka Doom *
D) 3*5*5*	Tek Ka Doom *	Tek Ka Tek Ka	Doom * Tek Ka	Tek Ka Doom *
E) 5*3*5*	Tek Ka Tek Ka	Doom * Tek Ka	Doom * Tek Ka	Tek Ka Doom

VERSE REPEAT

ENDING CHORUS

D) 3*5*5*	Tek Ka Doom *	Tek Ka Tek Ka	Doom * Tek Ka	Tek Ka Doom *
D) 3*5*5*	Tek Ka Doom *	Tek Ka Tek Ka	Doom * Tek Ka	Tek Ka Doom *
D) 3*5*5*	Tek Ka Doom *	Tek Ka Tek Ka	Doom * Tek Ka	Tek Ka Doom *
E) 5*3*5*	Tek Ka Tek Ka	Doom * Tek Ka	Doom * Tek Ka	Tek Ka Doom
Z) Singles*	Tek Ka Tek Ka	Tek Ka Tek Ka	Tek Ka Tek Ka	Tek Ka Tek Ka
Z) Singles*	Tek Ka Tek Ka	Tek Ka Tek Ka	Tek Ka Tek Ka	Tek Ka Doom

RHYTHM SONG LIBRARY

SECTION 3- SONG 18
DRUM NOTATION
Basic 3'S and 3*1*3*1*3* and 3*3*7* and 3*1*1*1*1*3* and 1*3*1*1*1*3*

VERSE

A) Basic 3's	Tek Ka Doom *	Tek Ka Doom *	Tek Ka Doom *	Tek Ka Doom *
B) 3*1*3*1*3*	Tek Ka Doom *	Doom * Tek Ka	Doom * Doom *	Tek Ka Doom *
B) 3*1*3*1*3*	Tek Ka Doom *	Doom * Tek Ka	Doom * Doom *	Tek Ka Doom *
C) 3*3*7*	Tek Ka Doom *	Tek Ka Doom *	Tek Ka Tek Ka	Tek Ka Doom *

CHORUS

D) 3*1*1*1*1*3*	Tek Ka Doom *	Doom * Doom *	Doom * Doom *	Tek Ka Doom *
D) 3*1*1*1*1*3*	Tek Ka Doom *	Doom * Doom *	Doom * Doom *	Tek Ka Doom *
E) 1*3*1*1*1*3*	Doom * Tek Ka	Doom * Doom *	Doom * Doom *	Tek Ka Doom *
D) 3*1*1*1*1*3*	Tek Ka Doom *	Doom * Doom *	Doom * Doom *	Tek Ka Doom *

VERSE REPEAT

ENDING CHORUS

D) 3*1*1*1*1*3*	Tek Ka Doom *	Doom * Doom *	Doom * Doom *	Tek Ka Doom *
D) 3*1*1*1*1*3*	Tek Ka Doom *	Doom * Doom *	Doom * Doom *	Tek Ka Doom *
E) 1*3*1*1*1*3*	Doom * Tek Ka	Doom * Doom *	Doom * Doom *	Tek Ka Doom *
D) 3*1*1*1*1*3*	Tek Ka Doom *	Doom * Doom *	Doom * Doom *	Tek Ka Doom *
Z) Singles*	Tek Ka Tek Ka	Tek Ka Tek Ka	Tek Ka Tek Ka	Tek Ka Tek Ka
Z) Singles*	Tek Ka Tek Ka	Tek Ka Tek Ka	Tek Ka Tek Ka	Tek Ka Doom

RHYTHM FACTORING

RHYTHM SONG LIBRARY

SECTION 3 SONG 19
DRUM NOTATION
3*5*1*3* and 5*1*1*1*3* and 5*5*3* and 5*1*5*1* and 5*1*7*

VERSE

A) 3*5*1*3*	Tek Ka Doom *	Tek Ka Tek Ka	Doom * Doom *	Tek Ka Doom *
B) 5*1*1*1*3*	Tek Ka Tek Ka	Doom * Doom *	Doom * Doom *	Tek Ka Doom *
C) 5*5*3*	Tek Ka Tek Ka	Doom * Tek Ka	Tek Ka Doom *	Tek Ka Doom *
B) 5*1*1*1*3*	Tek Ka Tek Ka	Doom * Doom *	Doom * Doom *	Tek Ka Doom *

CHORUS

D) 5*1*5*1*	Tek Ka Tek Ka	Doom * Doom *	Tek Ka Tek Ka	Doom * Doom *
E) 5*1*7*	Tek Ka Tek Ka	Doom * Doom *	Tek Ka Tek Ka	Tek Ka Doom *
D) 5*1*5*1*	Tek Ka Tek Ka	Doom * Doom *	Tek Ka Tek Ka	Doom * Doom *
E) 5*1*7*	Tek Ka Tek Ka	Doom * Doom *	Tek Ka Tek Ka	Tek Ka Doom *

VERSE REPEAT

ENDING CHORUS

D) 5*1*5*1*	Tek Ka Tek Ka	Doom * Doom *	Tek Ka Tek Ka	Doom * Doom *
E) 5*1*7*	Tek Ka Tek Ka	Doom * Doom *	Tek Ka Tek Ka	Tek Ka Doom *
D) 5*1*5*1*	Tek Ka Tek Ka	Doom * Doom *	Tek Ka Tek Ka	Doom * Doom *
E) 5*1*7*	Tek Ka Tek Ka	Doom * Doom *	Tek Ka Tek Ka	Tek Ka Doom *
Z) Singles*	Tek Ka Tek Ka	Tek Ka Tek Ka	Tek Ka Tek Ka	Tek Ka Tek Ka
Z) Singles*	Tek Ka Tek Ka	Tek Ka Tek Ka	Tek Ka Tek Ka	Tek Ka Doom

RHYTHM SONG LIBRARY

SECTION 4- SONG 20
SYNCOPATED 4's
Basic 3's and 3*4*4* and 5*4*3* and 7*1*4* and 3*1*3*4*

VERSE

A) Basic 3's	R L R *	R L R *	R L R *	R L R *
B) 3*4*4*	R L R *	R L ^ L	R * R L	^ L R *
B) 3*4*4*	R L R *	R L ^ L	R * R L	^ L R *
C) 5*4*3*	R L R L	R * R L	^ L R *	R L R *

CHORUS

D) 7*1*4*	R L R L	R L R *	R * R L	^ L R *
D) 7*1*4*	R L R L	R L R *	R * R L	^ L R *
D) 7*1*4*	R L R L	R L R *	R * R L	^ L R *
E) 3*1*3*4*	R L R *	R * R L	R * R L	^ L R *

VERSE REPEAT

ENDING CHORUS

D) 7*1*4*	R L R L	R L R *	R * R L	^ L R *
D) 7*1*4*	R L R L	R L R *	R * R L	^ L R *
D) 7*1*4*	R L R L	R L R *	R * R L	^ L R *
E) 3*1*3*4*	R L R *	R * R L	R * R L	^ L R *
Z) Singles*	R L R L	R L R L	R L R L	R L R L
Z) Singles*	R L R L	R L R L	R L R L	R L R *

RHYTHM SONG LIBRARY

SECTION 4- SONG 21
SYNCOPATED 4'S
5*1*4*1* and 3*4*1*3* and 7*1*4* and 4*4*1*1* and 3*1*4*1*1*

VERSE

A) 5*1*4*1*	R L R L	R * R *	R L ^ L	R * R *
B) 3*4*3*1*	R L R *	R L ^ L	R * R L	R * R *
A) 5*1*4*1*	R L R L	R * R *	R L ^ L	R * R *
A) 7*4*1*	R L R L	R L R *	R L ^ L	R * R *

CHORUS

C) 4*4*1*1*	R L ^ L	R * R L	^ L R *	R * R *
C) 4*4*1*1*	R L ^ L	R * R L	^ L R *	R * R *
D) 3*1*4*1*1*	R L R *	R * R L	^ L R *	R * R *
C) 4*4*1*1*	R L ^ L	R * R L	^ L R *	R * R *

VERSE REPEAT

ENDING CHORUS

C) 4*4*1*1*	R L ^ L	R * R L	^ L R *	R * R *
C) 4*4*1*1*	R L ^ L	R * R L	^ L R *	R * R *
D) 3*1*4*1*1*	R L R *	R * R L	^ L R *	R * R *
C) 4*4*1*1*	R L ^ L	R * R L	^ L R *	R * R *
Z) Singles*	R L R L	R L R L	R L R L	R L R L
Z) Singles*	R L R L	R L R L	R L R L	R L R *

RHYTHM FACTORING

RHYTHM SONG LIBRARY

SECTION 4 SONG 22
SYNCOPATED 2'S
Basic 2's and 2*5*5* and 3*2*2*3* and 3*2*3*1*1*

VERSE

A) Basic 2's	R R ^ *	R R ^ *	R R ^ *	R R ^ *
B) 2*5*5*	R R ^ *	R L R L	R * R L	R L R *
C) 2*3*1*5*	R R ^ *	R L R *	R * R L	R L R *
B) 2*5*5*	R R ^ *	R L R L	R * R L	R L R *

CHORUS

D) 3*2*2*3*	R L R *	R R ^ *	R R ^ *	R L R *
D) 3*2*2*3*	R L R *	R R ^ *	R R ^ *	R L R *
E) 3*2*7*	R L R *	R R ^ *	R L R L	R L R *
D) 3*2*2*3*	R L R *	R R ^ *	R R ^ *	R L R *

VERSE REPEAT

ENDING CHORUS

D) 3*2*2*3*	R L R *	R R ^ *	R R ^ *	R L R *
D) 3*2*2*3*	R L R *	R R ^ *	R R ^ *	R L R *
E) 3*2*7*	R L R *	R R ^ *	R L R L	R L R *
D) 3*2*2*3*	R L R *	R R ^ *	R R ^ *	R L R *
Z) Singles*	R L R L	R L R L	R L R L	R L R L
Z) Singles*	R L R L	R L R L	R L R L	R L R *

RHYTHM SONG LIBRARY

SECTION 4 SONG 23
SYNCOPATED 2'S
2*3*5*1 and 2*7*1*1 and 2*5*1*2* and 5*3*1*2*

VERSE

A) 2*7*1*1*	R R ^ *	R L R L	R L R *	R * R *
A) 2*7*1*1*	R R ^ *	R L R L	R L R *	R * R *
B) 2*7*2*	R R ^ *	R L R L	R L R *	R R ^ *
C) 3*2*3*1*1*	R L R *	R R ^ *	R L R *	R * R *

CHORUS

D) 2*5*1*2*	R R ^ *	R L R L	R * R *	R R ^ *
E) 2*1*1*2*2*	R L ^ *	R * R *	R R ^ *	R R ^ *
D) 2*5*1*2*	R R ^ *	R L R L	R * R *	R R ^ *
E) 2*1*1*2*2*	R L ^ *	R * R *	R R ^ *	R R ^ *

VERSE REPEAT

ENDING CHORUS

D) 2*5*1*2*	R R ^ *	R L R L	R * R *	R R ^ *
E) 2*1*1*2*2*	R L ^ *	R * R *	R R ^ *	R R ^ *
D) 2*5*1*2*	R R ^ *	R L R L	R * R *	R R ^ *
E) 2*1*1*2*2*	R L ^ *	R * R *	R R ^ *	R R ^ *
Z) Singles*	R L R L	R L R L	R L R L	R L R L
Z) Singles*	R L R L	R L R L	R L R L	R L R *

RHYTHM SONG LIBRARY

SECTION 4 SONG 24
SYNCOPATED 2'S & 4'S
2*4*5* and 4*1*2*3* and 2*5*5* and 2*2*7* and 2*3*7*

VERSE

A) 2*4*5*	R R ^ *	R L ^ L	R * R L	R L R *
A) 2*4*5*	R R ^ *	R L ^ L	R * R L	R L R *
B) 4*1*2*3*	R L ^ L	R * R *	R R ^ *	R L R *
C) 2*5*5*	R R ^ *	R L R L	R * R L	R L R *

CHORUS

D) 2*2*7*	R R ^ *	R R ^ *	R L R L	R L R *
E) 2*3*7*	R R ^ *	R L R *	R L R L	R L R *
D) 2*2*7*	R R ^ *	R R ^ *	R L R L	R L R *
E) 2*3*7*	R R ^ *	R L R *	R L R L	R L R *

VERSE REPEAT

ENDING CHORUS

D) 2*2*7*	R R ^ *	R R ^ *	R L R L	R L R *
E) 2*3*7*	R R ^ *	R L R *	R L R L	R L R *
D) 2*2*7*	R R ^ *	R R ^ *	R L R L	R L R *
E) 2*3*7*	R R ^ *	R L R *	R L R L	R L R *
Z) Singles*	R L R L	R L R L	R L R L	R L R L
Z) Singles*	R L R L	R L R L	R L R L	R L R *

RHYTHM FACTORING

RHYTHM SONG LIBRARY

SECTION 4 SONG 25
SYNCOPATED 2'S & 4'S
4*4*1*1* and 4*4*3* and 4*4*2* and 4*1*2*3* and 7*1*1*2* and 7*1*4*

VERSE

A) 4*4*1*1*	R L ^ L	R * R L	^ L R *	R * R *
B) 4*4*3*	R L ^ L	R * R L	^ L R *	R L R *
C) 4*4*2*	R L ^ L	R * R L	^ L R *	R R ^ *
D) 4*1*2*3*	R L ^ L	R * R *	R R ^ *	R L R *

CHORUS

E) 7*1*1*2*	R L R L	R L R *	R * R *	R R ^ *
F) 7*1*4*	R L R L	R L R *	R * R L	^ L R *
E) 7*1*1*2*	R L R L	R L R *	R * R *	R R ^ *
F) 7*1*4*	R L R L	R L R *	R * R L	^ L R *

VERSE REPEAT

ENDING CHORUS

E) 7*1*1*2*	R L R L	R L R *	R * R *	R R ^ *
F) 7*1*4*	R L R L	R L R *	R * R L	^ L R *
E) 7*1*1*2*	R L R L	R L R *	R * R *	R R ^ *
F) 7*1*4*	R L R L	R L R *	R * R L	^ L R *
Z) Singles*	R L R L	R L R L	R L R L	R L R L
Z) Singles*	R L R L	R L R L	R L R L	R L R *

RHYTHM FACTORING

RHYTHM SONG LIBRARY

SECTION 5- SONG 26
TIMING VARIATION 6 BEAT
Basic 3's and 3*7*3*7* and 3*7*5*1*3* and 3*3*3*7*3* and 7*7*7*

VERSE

A) Basic 3's	R L R *	R L R *	R L R *	R L R *	R L R *	R L R *
B) 3*7*3*7*	R L R *	R L R L	R L R L	R L R *	R L R L	R L R *
C) 3*7*5*1*3*	R L R *	R L R L	R L R *	R L R L	R * R *	R L R *
B) 3*7*3*7*	R L R *	R L R L	R L R L	R L R *	R L R L	R L R *

CHORUS

D) 3*3*3*7*3*	R L R *	R L R *	R L R *	R L R L	R L R *	R L R *
E) 3*3*3*7*3*	R L R *	R L R *	R L R *	R L R L	R L R *	R L R *
E) 7*7*7*	R L R L	R L R *	R L R L	R L R *	R L R L	R L R *
D) 7*7*7*	R L R L	R L R *	R L R L	R L R *	R L R L	R L R *

VERSE REPEAT

ENDING CHORUS

D) 3*3*3*7*3*	R L R *	R L R *	R L R *	R L R L	R L R *	R L R *
E) 3*3*3*7*3*	R L R *	R L R *	R L R *	R L R L	R L R *	R L R *
E) 7*7*7*	R L R L	R L R *	R L R L	R L R *	R L R L	R L R *
D) 7*7*7*	R L R L	R L R *	R L R L	R L R *	R L R L	R L R *
Z) Singles*	R L R L	R L R L	R L R L	R L R L	R L R L	R L R L
Z) Singles*	R L R L	R L R L	R L R L	R L R L	R L R L	R L R *

RHYTHM FACTORING

RHYTHM SONG LIBRARY

SECTION 5- SONG 27
TIMING VARIATION 6 BEAT
3*5*1*3*5*1* and 7*3*7*3* and 5*3*1*5*3*1* and 3*1*3*1*3*1*3*1* and 3*3*1*1*7*1*1*

VERSE

A) 3*5*1*3*5*1*	R L R *	R L R L	R * R *	R L R *	R L R L	R * R *
B) 7*3*7*3*	R L R L	R L R *	R L R *	R L R L	R L R *	R L R *
B) 7*3*7*3*	R L R L	R L R *	R L R *	R L R L	R L R *	R L R *
C) 5*3*1*5*3*1*	R L R L	R * R L	R * R *	R L R L	R * R L	R * R *

CHORUS

D) 3*1*3*1*3*1*3*1*	R L R *	R * R L	R * R *	R L R *	R * R L	R * R *
E) 3*3*1*1*7*1*1*	R L R *	R L R *	R * R *	R L R L	R L R *	R * R *
D) 3*1*3*1*3*1*3*1*	R L R *	R * R L	R * R *	R L R *	R * R L	R * R *
E) 3*3*1*1*7*1*1*	R L R *	R L R *	R * R *	R L R L	R L R *	R * R *

VERSE REPEAT

ENDING CHORUS

D) 3*1*3*1*3*1*3*1*	R L R *	R * R L	R * R *	R L R *	R * R L	R * R *
E) 3*3*1*1*7*1*1*	R L R *	R L R *	R * R *	R L R L	R L R *	R * R *
D) 3*1*3*1*3*1*3*1*	R L R *	R * R L	R * R *	R L R *	R * R L	R * R *
E) 3*3*1*1*7*1*1*	R L R *	R L R *	R * R *	R L R L	R L R *	R * R *
Z) Singles*	R L R L	R L R L	R L R L	R L R L	R L R L	R L R L
Z) Singles*	R L R L	R L R L	R L R L	R L R L	R L R L	R L R *

RHYTHM SONG LIBRARY

SECTION 5- SONG 28
TIMING VARIATION 6 BEAT
1*5*1*1*1*5*1*1* and 7*1*1*7*1*1* and1*3*1*3*1*7*1* and 3*3*3*1*1*3*3* and 3*7*5*1*3*

VERSE

A) 1*5*1*1*1*5*1*1*	R * R L	R L R *	R * R *	R * R L	R L R *	R * R *
B) 1*5*1*1*1*5*1*1*	R * R L	R L R *	R * R *	R * R L	R L R *	R * R *
B) 7*1*1*7*1*1*	R L R L	R L R *	R * R *	R L R L	R L R *	R * R *
C) 1*3*1*3*1*7*1*	R * R L	R * R *	R L R *	R * R L	R L R L	R * R *

CHORUS

D) 3*3*3*1*1*3*3*	R L R *	R L R *	R L R *	R * R *	R L R *	R L R *
E) 3*7*5*1*3*	R L R *	R L R L	R L R *	R L R L	R * R *	R L R *
E) 3*3*3*1*1*3*3*	R L R *	R L R *	R L R *	R * R *	R L R *	R L R *
D) 3*7*5*1*3*	R L R *	R L R L	R L R *	R L R L	R * R *	R L R *

VERSE REPEAT

ENDING CHORUS

D) 3*3*3*1*1*3*3*	R L R *	R L R *	R L R *	R * R *	R L R *	R L R *
E) 3*7*5*1*3*	R L R *	R L R L	R L R *	R L R L	R * R *	R L R *
E) 3*3*3*1*1*3*3*	R L R *	R L R *	R L R *	R * R *	R L R *	R L R *
D) 3*7*5*1*3*	R L R *	R L R L	R L R *	R L R L	R * R *	R L R *
Z) Singles*	R L R L	R L R L	R L R L	R L R L	R L R L	R L R L
Z) Singles*	R L R L	R L R L	R L R L	R L R L	R L R L	R L R *

RHYTHM SONG LIBRARY

SECTION 6- SONG 29
BIMANUAL DEXTERITY- RIGHT AND LEFT by factor
Basic 3'S and 3*3*7* and 7*7* and 3*5*5* and 5*3*5*

VERSE

A) Basic 3's	R L R *	L R L*	R L R *	L R L *
B) 3*3*7*	R L R *	L R L *	R L R L	R L R *
B) 3*3*7*	L R L *	R L R *	L R L R	L R L *
C) 7*7*	R L R L	R L R *	L R L R	L R L *

CHORUS

D) 3*5*5*	R L R *	L R L R	L * R L	R L R *
D) 3*5*5*	L R L *	R L R L	R * L R	L R L *
D) 3*5*5*	R L R *	L R L R	L * R L	R L R *
E) 5*3*5*	L R L R	L * R L	R * L R	L R L *

VERSE REPEAT

ENDING CHORUS

D) 3*5*5*	R L R *	L R L R	L * R L	R L R *
D) 3*5*5*	L R L *	R L R L	R * L R	L R L *
D) 3*5*5*	R L R *	L R L R	L * R L	R L R *
E) 5*3*5*	L R L R	L * R L	R * L R	L R L *
Z) Singles*	R L R L	R L R L	R L R L	R L R L
Z) Singles*	R L R L	R L R L	R L R L	R L R *

RHYTHM SONG LIBRARY

SECTION 6- SONG 30
BIMANUAL DEXTERITY- RIGHT AND LEFT by factor
Basic 3'S and 3*1*3*1*3* and 3*3*7* and 3*1*1*1*1*3* and 1*3*1*1*1*3*

VERSE

A) Basic 3's	R L R *	L R L *	R L R *	L R L *
B) 3*1*3*1*3*	R L R *	L * R L	R * L *	R L R *
B) 3*1*3*1*3*	L R L *	R * L R	L * R *	L R L *
C) 3*3*7*	R L R *	L R L *	R L R L	R L R *

CHORUS

D) 3*1*1*1*1*3*	L R L *	R * L *	R * L *	R L R *
D) 3*1*1*1*1*3*	R L R *	L * R *	L * R *	L R L *
E) 1*3*1*1*1*3*	R * L R	L * R *	L * R *	L R L *
D) 3*1*1*1*1*3*	R L R *	L * R *	L * R *	L R L *

VERSE REPEAT

ENDING CHORUS

D) 3*1*1*1*1*3*	L R L *	R * L *	R * L *	R L R *
D) 3*1*1*1*1*3*	R L R *	L * R *	L * R *	L R L *
E) 1*3*1*1*1*3*	R * L R	L * R *	L * R *	L R L *
D) 3*1*1*1*1*3*	R L R *	L * R *	L * R *	L R L *
Z) Singles*	R L R L	R L R L	R L R L	R L R L
Z) Singles*	R L R L	R L R L	R L R L	R L R *

RHYTHM FACTORING

RHYTHM SONG LIBRARY

SECTION 8- SONG 31
FINGER CYMBAL DANCE

FIGURE 1- BASIC FORWARD WALK

3*3*3*3*	R L R *	R L R *	R L R *	R L R *
3*3*3*3*	R L R *	R L R *	R L R *	R L R *
3*3*3*3*	R L R *	R L R *	R L R *	R L R *
3*3*3*3*	R L R *	R L R *	R L R *	R L R *

FIGURE 2- BACK CROSS COMBO

3*4*1*3*	R L R *	R L ^ L	R * R *	R L R *
3*4*1*3*	R L R *	R L ^ L	R * R *	R L R *
3*4*1*3*	R L R *	R L ^ L	R * R *	R L R *
SINGLES	R L R L	R L R L	R L R L	R L R *

FIGURE 3 ROLLING WALK ONE outer perimeter circle

MUFFLING- Finger cymbals held close to the body, thumbs wrap lower finger cymbal muting sound

MUFFLE ALL BEATS FOR THIS FIGURE

3*2*3*2*	R L R *	R R ^ *	R L R *	R R ^ *
3*2*3*2*	R L R *	R R ^ *	R L R *	R R ^ *
3*2*3*2*	R L R *	R R ^ *	R L R *	R R ^ *
3*2*3*2*	R L R *	R R ^ *	R L R *	R R ^ *

RHYTHM SONG LIBRARY

SECTION 8- SONG 31
FINGER CYMBAL DANCE- Continued

FIGURE 4 ROLLING WALK TWO- inner perimeter circle
PARTNERING TAPS- Finger cymbals held to side, accent beat played on neighbor's finger cymbals

3*3*3*tap*tap*	R L R *	R L R *	R L R *	TAP * TAP *
3*3*3*tap*tap*	R L R *	R L R *	R L R *	TAP * TAP *
3*3*3*tap*tap*	R L R *	R L R *	R L R *	TAP * TAP *
3*3*3*tap*tap*	R L R *	R L R *	R L R *	TAP * TAP *

FIGURE 5 ROLLING WALK THREE self-circle
    3TAPs COUPLING- tap thumb of one hand to the middle finger cymbal of the other hand.
    Finger cymbals are held overhead, accent beat is played on opposite thumb
        Touch right top finger cymbal to left bottom finger cymbal for accent notes
        RL- couple tap, RL- couple tap, RL- couple tap, RL-couple tap

3tap*3tap*3tap*3tap*	R L tap *	R L tap *	R L tap *	R L tap *
3tap*3tap*3tap*3tap*	R L tap *	R L tap *	R L tap *	R L tap *
3tap*3tap*3tap*3tap*	R L tap *	R L tap *	R L tap *	R L tap *
3tap*3tap*3tap*3tap*	R L tap *	R L tap *	R L tap *	R L tap *

FIGURE 6 DOUBLE CROSS BASIC- Forward Walk

3*7*3*	R L R *	R L R L	R L R *	R L R *
3*7*3*	R L R *	R L R L	R L R *	R L R *
3*7*3*	R L R *	R L R L	R L R *	R L R *
3*7*3*	R L R *	R L R L	R L R *	R L R *

RHYTHM SONG LIBRARY

SECTION 8- SONG 31
FINGER CYMBAL DANCE- Continued

FIGURE 7 ROCKING HORSE- Inner Perimeter Circle
  3TAPS High and Low
  3TAPs tap thumb finger cymbal of one hand to the middle finger cymbal of the other hand.

    High 3TAPs - Finger cymbals held overhead, accent beat is played on opposite thumb
    Low 3TAPs - Finger cymbals are behind back, accent beat is played on opposite thumb
    RL- Side, RL- High, RL- Side, RL-Low

3TAP High and Low	R L R(Side) *	R L (H)tap *	R L R(Side) *	R L (L)tap *
3TAP High and Low	R L R(Side) *	R L (H)tap *	R L R(Side) *	R L (L)tap *
3TAP High and Low	R L R(Side) *	R L (H)tap *	R L R(Side) *	R L (L)tap *
3TAP High and Low	R L R(Side) *	R L (H)tap *	R L R(Side) *	R L (L)tap *

FIGURE 8- ROCKING HORSE- Quarter Turn Self Circle
  3TAPS High and Low
  3TAPs tap thumb finger cymbal of one hand to the middle finger cymbal of the other hand.
  SAME AS FIGURE 7 ABOVE

3TAP High and Low	R L R(Side) *	R L (H)tap *	R L R(Side) *	R L (L)tap *
3TAP High and Low	R L R(Side) *	R L (H)tap *	R L R(Side) *	R L (L)tap *
3TAP High and Low	R L R(Side) *	R L (H)tap *	R L R(Side) *	R L (L)tap *
3TAP High and Low	R L R(Side) *	R L (H)tap *	R L R(Side) *	R L (L)tap *

FIGURE 9- FIVES FORWARD

3*3*7*	R L R *	R L R *	R L R L	R L R *
3*3*7*	R L R *	R L R *	R L R L	R L R *
3*3*7*	R L R *	R L R *	R L R L	R L R *
3*3*7*	R L R *	R L R *	R L R L	R L R *

RHYTHM FACTORING

RHYTHM SONG LIBRARY

SECTION 8- SONG 31
FINGER CYMBAL DANCE- Continued

FIGURE 10- FIVES TWIST

3*3*7*	R L R *	R L R *	R L R L	R L R *
3*3*7*	R L R *	R L R *	R L R L	R L R *
3*3*7*	R L R *	R L R *	R L R L	R L R *
3*3*7*	R L R *	R L R *	R L R L	R L R *

FIGURE 11- FIVES TURNING

3*3*7*	R L R *	R L R *	R L R L	R L R *
3*3*7*	R L R *	R L R *	R L R L	R L R *
3*3*7*	R L R *	R L R *	R L R L	R L R *
3*3*7*	R L R *	R L R *	R L R L	R L R *

FIGURE 12- TRAVELING GRAPEVINE

PARTNERING TAPS- 1*3*3*TAPs-
Finger cymbals held out to side, accent beat is played on neighbor's finger cymbals
Touch both right finger cymbals to right neighbor's finger cymbals
Touch both left finger cymbals to left neighbor's finger cymbals

* 1*3*3*TAPS	* * R *	R L R *	R L R *	TAP * TAP *
* 1*3*3*TAPS	* * R *	R L R *	R L R *	TAP * TAP *
* 1*3*3*TAPS	* * R *	R L R *	R L R *	TAP * TAP *
* 1*3*3*TAPS	* * R *	R L R *	R L R *	TAP * TAP *

FINAL FIGURE- GOOSH SPIN

SINGLES	R L R L	R L R L	R L R L	R L R L

SECTION 8

FINGER CYMBAL DANCE

FINGER CYMBAL DANCE

INTRODUCTION TO FINGER CYMBAL DANCE
The Finger Cymbal Dance is a traveling circle group dance. It is best to start with a basic understanding of the dance forms, then add finger cymbal complexities. The arm movements correlate to the steps and the rhythm patterns blend with the steps to form musical movement texture.

GROUP CIRCLE FORMS
Group Circle- dancers move around center of group circle
Self-Circle- individual dancers circle around themselves
Moving Group Circle- group moves together in one direction
    Inner Perimeter Circle- facing toward Center, sideways motion around circle
    Outer Perimeter Circle- facing away from Center, sideways motion around circle

DANCE CALLER
It is helpful to have a "caller," someone who is not participating in the dance to watch the positioning of the circle and call transitions from one figure to the next.

DANCE FORMATIONS
BASIC FORWARD WALK SEQUENCE- Basics, Cross-Basic, Backcross Combo
ROLLING WALK SEQUENCE- Rolling Walk One, Two Three and Goosh Spin
ROCKING HORSE COMBO- Rocking Horse Step, Rocking Horse Turn
FIVES SEQUENCE- Fives, Fives Twist, Fives Turn
GRAPEVINE- Traveling Twist Step- Inner/Outer Perimeter Circle

FRAMING ARM POSTURES
Framing involves the position of the arms around the movement of the body. If the body is facing full forward, the arms are held out and up evenly on both sides. If the movement is toward the right, the left arm will be fully elevated while the right arms is held out toward the right. If the movement is toward the left, the right arm will be elevated while the left arm is held out toward the left

Example- FIGURE 6- DOUBLE CROSS BASIC (walking circle) 3*7*3* framing
Example- FIGURE 9- FIVES STRAIGHT (Inner Perimeter circle) 3*3*7* framing
Example- FIGURE 10- FIVES TWIST (Outer Perimeter circle) 3*3*7* framing
Example- FIGURE 11- FIVES TURN (Self circle) 3*3*7* framing

RHYTHM FACTORING

FINGER CYMBAL DANCE

SPECIAL FINGER CYMBAL TONES

When dancing with finger cymbals, coordinated movements and simple rhythm phrases combine to create new sounds. By pairing simple steps with special finger cymbal tones, this group circle dance can turn simple patterns into a playful, interactive exercise. There are several ways to play finger cymbals that are distinct to the Finger Cymbal Dance. Special tones are created by playing a familiar pattern with simple coordinated movement variation.

MUFFLING

Muffled notes are played by cupping the cymbals, so the skin of the palm braces the inner edges of both finger cymbals creating a quieter and smoother tone than standard playing.
Example- FIGURE 3- ROLLING WALK ONE (Outer Perimeter circle) 3*2*3*2* muffled

3TAPs COUPLING TAPS

3TAPs- tap thumb cymbal of one hand to middle cymbal of other hand.

The simplest form is played in front of the body.

Variations include overhead or behind the back.

Example- FIGURE 5- ROLLING WALK THREE (Self circle) 3tap* overhead

Example- FIGURE 7- ROCKING HORSE (Inner perimeter circle) 3tap* high-low

Example- FIGURE 8- ROCKING HORSE TURN (self-circle) 3tap* high-low

PARTNERING TAPS

Partnering and group dynamics add more variation to the Finger Cymbal Dance, adding new tones and movement coordination by playing off a neighbor's finger cymbals. These special notes sound different than all others due to the position of the hands. This involves opening the hands wide and tapping thumb cymbal into neighbor's thumb cymbal while tapping middle cymbal to neighbors middle cymbal.

Example- FIGURE 4- ROLLING WALK TWO (Inner perimeter circle) 3*tap*tap coupled

Example- FIGURE 12- GRAPEVINE (Inner perimeter circle) 1*3*3*tap*tap* coupled**

FINGER CYMBAL DANCE

FINGER CYMBAL DANCE FIGURE BY FIGURE

FIGURE 1- BASIC FORWARD WALK(Walking circle)	Basic 3's
FIGURE 2- BACK CROSS COMBO- (Inner perimeter circle)	3*4*1*3*
FIGURE 3- ROLLING WALK ONE (Outer perimeter circle)	3*2*3*2* muffled
FIGURE 4- ROLLING WALK TWO (Inner perimeter circle)	3*tap*tap coupled
FIGURE 5- ROLLING WALK THREE (Self circle)	3tap* overhead
FIGURE 6- DOUBLE CROSS BASIC (walking circle)	3*7*3* framing
FIGURE 7- ROCKING HORSE (Inner perimeter circle)	3tap* high and low
FIGURE 8- ROCKING HORSE TURN (self-circle)	3tap* high and low
FIGURE 9- FIVES STRAIGHT (Inner perimeter circle)	3*3*7* framing
FIGURE 10- FIVES TWIST (Outer perimeter circle)	3*3*7* framing
FIGURE 11- FIVES TURN (Self circle)	3*3*7* framing
FIGURE 12- GRAPEVINE (Inner perimeter circle)	1*3*3***tap*tap* coupled
FINAL FIGURE- GOOSH SPIN (Rolling Walk 4 turning)	Singles

FINGER CYMBAL DANCE

FIGURE 1

BASIC FORWARD WALK- Step touch

Forward walking step in group circle moving clockwise

BASIC FORWARD WALK

Step forward onto right foot

Drag left foot forward touching toes to ground at right heel

Accent toss left hip as left toes touch down at right heel

Step forward onto left foot

Drag right foot forward touching toes to ground at left heel

Accent toss right hip as left toes touch down at left heel

Repeat movements- Step touch, Step touch, Step touch, Step touch

BASIC FORWARD WALK- Step touch

3*3*3*3*	R L R *	R L R *	R L R *	R L R *
Step Touch	Step right	Touch left	Step left	Touch right
3*3*3*3*	R L R *	R L R *	R L R *	R L R *
Step Touch	Step right	Touch left	Step left	Touch right
3*3*3*3*	R L R *	R L R *	R L R *	R L R *
Step Touch	Step right	Touch left	Step left	Touch right
3*3*3*3*	R L R *	R L R *	R L R *	R L R *
Step Touch	Step right	Touch left	Step left	Touch right

FINGER CYMBAL DANCE

FIGURE 2

BACK CROSS COMBO- Inner perimeter back step cross touch

Facing toward center of group circle, moving side to side with back cross combo movement

BACK CROSS COMBO

Back Cross Right-

Step to the back on right foot, crossing right leg behind left foot

Step to the left-on-left foot, opening stance with step

Step to the front on right foot, crossing right leg in front of left foot

Touch left toes to ground beside right foot, accent with left hip toss

Back Cross Left-

Repeat toward left

Back Cross Right

Repeat toward right- modified swing left leg around to front instead of accent

Front Cross Left-

Swing left leg around for front cross moving toward the right

Step open stance onto right leg

Step to the back on left foot

Touch right toes to ground beside left foot, accent with right hip toss

BACK CROSS COMBO- Inner perimeter back step cross touch

3*4*1*3*	R L R *	R L ^ L	R * R *	R L R *
Back Cross Right	Right Step back	Left Step open	Right Step front	Left touch
3*4*1*3*	R L R *	R L ^ L	R * R *	R L R *
Back Cross Left	Left Step back	Right Step open	Left Step front	Right touch
3*4*1*3*	R L R *	R L ^ L	R * R *	R L R *
Back Cross Right	Right Step back	Left Step open	Right Step front	Left swing around
SINGLES	R L R L	R L R L	R L R L	R L R *
Front Cross Left	Left Step front	Right Step open	Left Step back	Right touch

FINGER CYMBAL DANCE

FIGURE 3

ROLLING STEP ONE- Outer perimeter circle creeping limp step

Facing outward from center of group circle, group moving counterclockwise together

ROLLING STEP ONE

Step onto right foot, chest pulse forward

Limp Step on left foot, chest fall back- drag left foot, left toes to right heel

Step onto right foot, chest pulse forward

Limp Step on left foot, chest fall back- drag left foot, left toes to right heel

Repeat leading each time on right foot, dragging left foot in limping walk

MUFFLING- Cymbals held close to the body, thumbs wrap around lower cymbal muting sound

ROLLING STEP ONE- Outer perimeter circle creeping limp step

3*2*3*2*	R L R *	R R ^ *	R L R *	R R ^ *
ROLL one	Right Step	Left drag	Right Step	Left drag
3*2*3*2*	R L R *	R R ^ *	R L R *	R R ^ *
ROLL one	Right Step	Left drag	Right Step	Left drag
3*2*3*2*	R L R *	R R ^ *	R L R *	R R ^ *
ROLL one	Right Step	Left drag	Right Step	Left drag
3*2*3*2*	R L R *	R R ^ *	R L R *	R R ^ *
ROLL one	Right Step	Left drag	Right Step	Left drag

FINGER CYMBAL DANCE

FIGURE 4

ROLLING WALK TWO- Inner perimeter circle limping side sway

Facing inward toward center of circle, shifting slightly left and right together

ROLLING WALK TWO

Step onto right foot, elevate onto toes, raised chest pulse forward

Weight shift back on left foot, chest fall back

Step open toward right-on-right foot tippy toes, raised chest pulse forward

Weight shift on left foot tippy toes, chest fall back-

Repeat sequence continuing to lead with right foot

PARTNERING TAPS- Finger cymbals out to side, accent played on neighbor's finger cymbals

Touch right top and bottom finger cymbals to right neighbor's top and bottom finger cymbals

Touch left top and bottom finger cymbals to left neighbor's top and bottom finger cymbals

RLR-, RLR, RLR coupled tap tap

ROLLING WALK TWO- Inner perimeter circle limping side sway

3*3*3*tap*tap*	R L R *	R L R *	R L R *	tap * tap *
ROLL two	Right Cross	Left Shift	Right open tippy toes	Left tippy toes
3*3*3*tap*tap*	R L R *	R L R *	R L R *	tap * tap *
ROLL two	Right Cross	Left Shift	Right open tippy toes	Left tippy toes
3*3*3*tap*tap*	R L R *	R L R *	R L R *	tap * tap *
ROLL two	Right Cross	Left Shift	Right open tippy toes	Left tippy toes
3*3*3*tap*tap*	R L R *	R L R *	R L R *	tap * tap *
ROLL two	Right Cross	Left Shift	Right open tippy toes	Left tippy toes

RHYTHM FACTORING

FINGER CYMBAL DANCE

FIGURE 5

ROLLING WALK THREE- Self-circle limping turn

Circle around self, one quarter rotation per line

ROLLING WALK THREE

Step onto right foot, chest pulse forward

Limp Step on left foot, chest fall back- drag left foot, left toes to right heel

Step onto right foot, chest pulse forward

Limp Step on left foot, chest fall back- drag left foot, left hip swing rotating left

Body rotate ¼ turn clockwise with each ROLLING WALK sequence

Repeat leading each time on right foot, rotating around in complete circle

3TAPs COUPLING- tap the thumb of one hand to the middle finger cymbal of the other hand.
Finger cymbals held overhead, accent beat is played on opposite thumb

Touch right top finger cymbal to left bottom finger cymbal for accent notes

RL- couple tap, RL- couple tap, RL- couple tap, RL-couple tap

ROLLING WALK THREE- Self-circle limping turn

3tap*3tap*3tap*3tap*	R L tap *	R L tap *	R L tap *	R L tap *
ROLL three	Right Step	Left drag	Right Step	Left rotate
3tap*3tap*3tap*3tap*	R L tap *	R L tap *	R L tap *	R L tap *
ROLL three	Right Step	Left drag	Right Step	Left rotate
3tap*3tap*3tap*3tap*	R L tap *	R L tap *	R L tap *	R L tap *
ROLL three	Right Step	Left drag	Right Step	Left rotate
3tap*3tap*3tap*3tap*	R L tap *	R L tap *	R L tap *	R L tap *
ROLL three	Right Step	Left drag	Right Step	Left rotate

FINGER CYMBAL DANCE

FIGURE 6

DOUBLE CROSS BASIC- Forward walk cross combo

Forward walking cross step in group circle moving clockwise

DOUBLE CROSS BASIC

Step forward onto right foot toward the left crossing in front of left foot

Step forward onto left foot next to right foot

Step forward again on right foot toward the left crossing in front of left foot

Drag left foot forward touching toes to ground beside right foot

Accent toss left hip as left toes touch down at right heel

Repeat sequence starting with left foot crossing toward the right

FRAMING- Arms held up and out to sides with lead arm lower than following arm

As the right foot leads crossing toward the left, the movement is toward the left and the left arm is the lead arm. Left arm held out at shoulder height while right arm held overhead.

As the left foot leads crossing toward the right, the movement is toward the right and the right arm is the lead arm. Right arm held out a shoulder height while left arm held overhead.

DOUBLE CROSS BASIC- Forward walk cross combo

3*7*3*	R L R *	R L R L	R L R *	R L R *
Double Cross Basic	Cross Step right	Step left	Cross Step right	Touch left
3*7*3*	R L R *	R L R L	R L R *	R L R *
Double Cross Basic	Cross Step left	Step right	Cross Step left	Touch right
3*7*3*	R L R *	R L R L	R L R *	R L R *
Double Cross Basic	Cross Step right	Step left	Cross Step right	Touch left
3*7*3*	R L R *	R L R L	R L R *	R L R *
Double Cross Basic	Cross Step left	Step right	Cross Step left	Touch right

RHYTHM FACTORING

FINGER CYMBAL DANCE

FIGURE 7

ROCKING HORSE- Inner perimeter circle rocking step combo

Facing toward center of circle, rocking in toward center and rocking back away from center

ROCKING HORSE

Step forward onto right foot

Touch forward left foot next to right foot

Accent by swinging hips forward with toe touch, leaning slightly back at waist

Step back onto right foot

Touch back left foot next to right foot

Accent by swinging hips back with toe touch, leaning slightly forward at waist

3TAPS COUPLING- High and Low

3TAPs- tap thumb cymbal of one hand to the middle cymbal of the other hand.

> **High 3TAPs** - Finger cymbals held over head, accent beat played on opposite thumb
> **Low 3TAPs** - Finger cymbals behind back, accent beat played on opposite thumb
> RL- Side, RL- High, RL- Side, RL-Low

ROCKING HORSE- Inner perimeter circle rocking step combo

3TAP High and Low	R L Side *	R L (H)tap *	R L Side *	R L (L)tap *
Rocking Horse	Step Fwd Right	Touch Fwd Left	Step Back Right	Touch Back Left
3TAP High and Low	R L Side *	R L (H)tap *	R L Side *	R L (L)tap *
Rocking Horse	Step Fwd Right	Touch Fwd Left	Step Back Right	Touch Back Left
3TAP High and Low	R L Side *	R L (H)tap *	R L Side *	R L (L)tap *
Rocking Horse	Step Fwd Right	Touch Fwd Left	Step Back Right	Touch Back Left
3TAP High and Low	R L Side *	R L (H)tap *	R L Side *	R L (L)tap *
Rocking Horse	Step Fwd Right	Touch Fwd Left	Step Back Right	Touch Back Left

FINGER CYMBAL DANCE

FIGURE 8

ROCKING HORSE- Quarter turn self-circle rocking step combo

Facing toward Center of circle, with each Back Rock, Pivot ¼ Turn toward the left

ROCKING HORSE

Step forward onto right foot

Touch forward left foot next to right foot

Accent by swinging hips forward with toe touch leaning slightly back at waist

Step back onto right foot

Touch back left foot next to right foot

Pivot ¼ Turn toward the left

3TAPS COUPLING- High and Low

3TAPs- tap thumb cymbal of one hand to the middle cymbal of the other hand.

> **High 3TAPs** - Finger cymbals held over head, accent beat played on opposite thumb
> **Low 3TAPs** - Finger cymbals behind back, accent beat played on opposite thumb
> RL- Side, RL- High, RL- Side, RL-Low

ROCKING HORSE- Quarter turn self-circle rocking step combo

3TAP High and Low	R L Side *	R L (H)tap *	R L Side *	R L (L)tap *
Rocking Horse ¼ Turn	Step Fwd Right	Touch Fwd Left	Step Back Right	Touch Pivot Left
3TAP High and Low	R L Side *	R L (H)tap *	R L Side *	R L (L)tap *
Rocking Horse ¼ Turn	Step Fwd Right	Touch Fwd Left	Step Back Right	Touch Pivot Left
3TAP High and Low	R L Side *	R L (H)tap *	R L Side *	R L (L)tap *
Rocking Horse ¼ Turn	Step Fwd Right	Touch Fwd Left	Step Back Right	Touch Pivot Left
3TAP High and Low	R L Side *	R L (H)tap *	R L Side *	R L (L)tap *
Rocking Horse ¼ Turn	Step Fwd Right	Touch Fwd Left	Step Back Right	Touch Pivot Left

FINGER CYMBAL DANCE

FIGURE 9

FIVES PROGRESSION- FIVES FORWARD

Facing toward center of circle

FIVES FORWARD- Slow, Slow, quick, quick, quick,

FIVES RIGHT

Shift weight back on right foot rocking slightly back, slow Step
Shift weight forward onto left foot, slow Step
Scoot toward the right on right foot- quick Step
Scoot toward the right on left foot- quick Step
Scoot toward the right on the right foot- quick Step

FIVES LEFT

Shift weight back on left foot rocking slightly back- slow Step
Step forward onto right foot- slow Step
Scoot toward the left on left foot- quick Step
Scoot toward the left on right foot- quick Step
Scoot toward the left on left foot- quick Step

FIVES FORWARD

3*3*7*	R L R *	R L R *	R L R L	R L R *
Fives Right	Rock Back Right	Step Forward Left	Scoot Right	Scoot Left Scoot Right
3*3*7*	R L R *	R L R *	R L R L	R L R *
Fives Left	Rock Back Left	Step Forward Right	Scoot Left	Scoot Right Scoot Left
3*3*7*	R L R *	R L R *	R L R L	R L R *
Fives Right	Rock Back Right	Step Forward Left	Scoot Right	Scoot Left Scoot Right
3*3*7*	R L R *	R L R *	R L R L	R L R *
Fives Left	Rock Back Left	Step Forward Right	Scoot Left	Scoot Right Scoot Left

RHYTHM FACTORING

FINGER CYMBAL DANCE

FIGURE 10

FIVES PROGRESSION- FIVES TWIST

Facing toward center of circle

FIVES TWIST- Slow, Slow, quick, quick, quick,

FIVES RIGHT with Twist

Step back on right foot rocking back and twist to look over right shoulder, slow Step
Step forward onto left foot, slow Step
Scoot toward the right on right foot- quick Step
Scoot toward the right on left foot- quick Step
Scoot toward the right on the right foot- quick Step

FIVES LEFT with Twist

Step back on left foot rocking back and twist to look over left shoulder- slow Step
Step forward onto right foot- slow Step
Scoot toward the left on left foot- quick Step
Scoot toward the left on right foot- quick Step
Scoot toward the left on left foot- quick Step

FIVES TWIST

3*3*7*	R L R *	R L R *	R L R L	R L R *
Fives Right	Twist Back Right	Step Forward Left	Scoot Right	Scoot Left Scoot Right
3*3*7*	R L R *	R L R *	R L R L	R L R *
Fives Left	Twist Back Left	Step Forward Right	Scoot Left	Scoot Right Scoot Left
3*3*7*	R L R *	R L R *	R L R L	R L R *
Fives Right	Twist Back Right	Step Forward Left	Scoot Right	Scoot Left Scoot Right
3*3*7*	R L R *	R L R *	R L R L	R L R *
Fives Left	Twist Back Left	Step Forward Right	Scoot Left	Scoot Right Scoot Left

FINGER CYMBAL DANCE

FIGURE 11

FIVES PROGRESSION- FIVES TURNING

Facing toward center of circle

FIVES TURNING Slow, Slow, quick, quick, quick,

FIVES RIGHT- Turning to the Left

Step back on right foot rocking weight back onto right leg, slow Step
Step forward onto left foot, slow Step
Step across with right foot crossing in front of left foot- quick Step
Turning Step continuing toward the left on left foot- quick Step
Turning Step continuing toward the left on right foot to complete the turn- quick Step

FIVES LEFT- Turning to the Right

Step back on left foot rocking weight back onto left leg- slow Step
Step forward onto right foot- slow Step
Scoot toward the left on left foot- quick Step
Scoot toward the left on right foot- quick Step
Scoot toward the left on left foot- quick Step

FIVES TURNING

3*3*7*	R L R *	R L R *	R L R L	R L R *
Fives Right	Rock Back Right	Step Forward Left	Cross Step Right	Turn Step Left Right
3*3*7*	R L R *	R L R *	R L R L	R L R *
Fives Left	Rock Back Left	Step Forward Right	Cross Step Left	Turn Step Right Left
3*3*7*	R L R *	R L R *	R L R L	R L R *
Fives Right	Rock Back Right	Step Forward Left	Cross Step Right	Turn Step Left Right
3*3*7*	R L R *	R L R *	R L R L	R L R *
Fives Left	Rock Back Left	Step Forward Right	Cross Step Left	Turn Step Right Left

FINGER CYMBAL DANCE

FIGURE 12

TRAVELING GRAPEVINE

Facing toward center of circle, group moves together clockwise

TRAVELING GRAPEVINE

Step to the back on right foot, crossing right leg behind left foot
Step to the left on left foot, opening stance with Step
Step to the front on right foot, crossing right leg in front of left foot
Step to the left on left foot, opening stance with Step

PARTNERING TAPS- 1*3*3*TAPs-

Finger cymbals out to side, accent beat played on neighbor's finger cymbals
Touch right finger cymbals to right neighbor's top and bottom finger cymbals
Touch left finger cymbals to left neighbor's top and bottom finger cymbals
R * RLR * RLR * TAP, TAP- coupling taps with neighbor

TRAVELING GRAPEVINE

1*3*3*TAPS	R * R L	R * R L	R * * *	TAP * TAP *
Back Cross Right	Right Step Back	Left Step Open	Right Step Front	Left Step Open
1*3*3*TAPS	R * R L	R * R L	R * * *	TAP * TAP *
Back Cross Right	Right Step Back	Left Step Open	Right Step Front	Left Step Open
1*3*3*TAPS	R * R L	R * R L	R * * *	TAP * TAP *
Back Cross Right	Right Step Back	Left Step Open	Right Step Front	Left Step Open
1*3*3*TAPS	R * R L	R * R L	R * * *	TAP * TAP *
Back Cross Right	Right Step Back	Left Step Open	Right Step Front	Left Step Open

FINGER CYMBAL DANCE

FINAL FIGURE

GOOSH SPIN

Facing toward Center, circling around self progressively faster to finish

GOOSH SPIN-

ROLLING WALK TWO TURNING

GOOSH Step onto right foot, pressing down into ground, thrusting right hip outward

Limp Step on left foot, turning slightly toward the right- clockwise

Step toward right on right foot tippy toes, chest pulse forward

Step on left foot tippy toes, turning slightly toward the right- clockwise

Repeat sequence continuing to lead with right foot

Turn clockwise with each Step sequence, gradually increasing the speed of turning

Spin faster and faster, with GOOSH downward accent and elevation turning

GOOSH SPIN

SINGLES	R L R L	R L R L	R L R L	R L R L
ROLL Two	GOOSH Step right	Left drag	Right tippy toes	Left tippy toes
SINGLES	R L R L	R L R L	R L R L	R L R L
ROLL Two	GOOSH Step right	Left drag	Right tippy toes	Left tippy toes
SINGLES	R L R L	R L R L	R L R L	R L R L
ROLL Two	GOOSH Step right	Left drag	Right tippy toes	Left tippy toes
SINGLES	R L R L	R L R L	R L R L	R L R *
ROLL Two	GOOSH Step right	Left drag	Right tippy toes	Left tippy toes

OTHER WORKS BY THE AUTHOR

THERAPEUTIC EMBODIMENT PRACTICES

SPIN AND FLOW

Illustrated guide to integrated implement training and fusion flow arts

THE ART OF THE LULLABY

Vocal coaching for comfort care

EDUCATIONAL WORKBOOKS AND COLORING BOOKS

MIND MAPPING

Illustration tools for integrating complex thoughts and emotions

WELLNESS CHARTING

Self-care coloring workbook tracking 100 wellness behaviors

WOMB WISDOM

Childbirth preparation coloring workbook

ENSHROUDED

End of life preparation and grief processing coloring workbook

HOSPICE EARTH

Environmental crisis awareness coloring book featuring news headlines